FILMMAKERS SERIES

edited by
Anthony Slide

1. *James Whale*, by James Curtis. 1982
2. *Cinema Stylists*, by John Belton. 1983
3. *Harry Langdon*, by William Schelly. 1982
4. *William A. Wellman*, by Frank Thompson. 1983
5. *Stanley Donen*, by Joseph Casper. 1983
6. *Brian De Palma*, by Michael Bliss. 1983
7. *J. Stuart Blackton*, by Marian Blackton Trimble. 1985
8. *Martin Scorsese and Michael Cimino*, by Michael Bliss. 1985
9. *Franklin J. Schaffner*, by Erwin Kim. 1985
10. *D.W. Griffith and the Biograph Company*, by Cooper C. Graham et al. 1985
11. *Some Day We'll Laugh: An Autobiography*, by Esther Ralston. 1985
12. *The Memoirs of Alice Guy Blaché*, 2nd ed., translated by Roberta and Simone Blaché. 1996
13. *Leni Riefenstahl and Olympia*, by Cooper C. Graham. 1986
14. *Robert Florey*, by Brian Taves. 1987
15. *Henry King's America*, by Walter Coppedge. 1986
16. *Aldous Huxley and Film*, by Virginia M. Clark. 1987
17. *Five American Cinematographers*, by Scott Eyman. 1987
18. *Cinematographers on the Art and Craft of Cinematography*, by Anna Kate Sterling. 1987
19. *Stars of the Silents*, by Edward Wagenknecht. 1987
20. *Twentieth Century-Fox*, by Aubrey Solomon. 1988
21. *Highlights and Shadows: The Memoirs of a Hollywood Cameraman*, by Charles G. Clarke. 1989
22. *I Went That-a-Way: The Memoirs of a Western Film Director*, by Harry L. Fraser; edited by Wheeler Winston Dixon and Audrey Brown Fraser. 1990
23. *Order in the Universe: The Films of John Carpenter*, by Robert C. Cumbow. 1990 *(out of print; see No. 70)*
24. *The Films of Freddie Francis*, by Wheeler Winston Dixon. 1991
25. *Hollywood Be Thy Name*, by William Bakewell. 1991

26. *The Charm of Evil: The Life and Films of Terence Fisher,* by Wheeler Winston Dixon. 1991
27. *Lionheart in Hollywood: The Autobiography of Henry Wilcoxon,* with Katherine Orrison. 1991
28. *William Desmond Taylor: A Dossier,* by Bruce Long. 1991
29. *The Films of Leni Riefenstahl,* 2nd ed., by David B. Hinton. 1991
30. *Hollywood Holyland: The Filming and Scoring of "The Greatest Story Ever Told,"* by Ken Darby. 1992
31. *The Films of Reginald LeBorg: Interviews, Essays, and Filmography,* by Wheeler Winston Dixon. 1992
32. *Memoirs of a Professional Cad,* by George Sanders, with Tony Thomas. 1992
33. *The Holocaust in French Film,* by André Pierre Colombat. 1993
34. *Robert Goldstein and "The Spirit of '76,"* edited and compiled by Anthony Slide. 1993
35. *Those Were the Days, My Friend: My Life in Hollywood with David O. Selznick and Others,* by Paul Macnamara. 1993
36. *The Creative Producer,* by David Lewis, edited by James Curtis. 1993
37. *Reinventing Reality: The Art and Life of Rouben Mamoulian,* by Mark Spergel. 1993
38. *Malcolm St. Clair: His Films, 1915–1948,* by Ruth Anne Dwyer. 1997
39. *Beyond Hollywood's Grasp: American Filmmakers Abroad, 1914–1945,* by Harry Waldman. 1994
40. *A Steady Digression to a Fixed Point,* by Rose Hobart. 1994
41. *Radical Juxtaposition: The Films of Yvonne Rainer,* by Shelley Green. 1994
42. *Company of Heroes: My Life as an Actor in the John Ford Stock Company,* by Harry Carey Jr. 1994
43. *Strangers in Hollywood: A History of Scandinavian Actors in American Films from 1910 to World War II,* by Hans J. Wollstein. 1994
44. *Charlie Chaplin: Intimate Close-Ups,* by Georgia Hale, edited with an introduction and notes by Heather Kiernan. 1995
45. *The Word Made Flesh: Catholicism and Conflict in the Films of Martin Scorsese,* by Michael Bliss. 1995
46. *W. S. Van Dyke's Journal: White Shadows in the South Seas (1927–1928) and other Van Dyke on Van Dyke,* edited and annotated by Rudy Behlmer. 1996

47. *Music from the House of Hammer: Music in the Hammer Horror Films, 1950–1980,* by Randall D. Larson. 1996
48. *Directing: Learn from the Masters,* by Tay Garnett. 1996
49. *Featured Player: An Oral Autobiography of Mae Clarke,* edited with an introduction by James Curtis. 1996
50. *A Great Lady: A Life of the Screenwriter Sonya Levien,* by Larry Ceplair. 1996
51. *A History of Horrors: The Rise and Fall of the House of Hammer,* by Denis Meikle. 1996
52. *The Films of Michael Powell and the Archers,* by Scott Salwolke. 1997
53. *From Oz to E.T.: Wally Worsley's Half-Century in Hollywood—A Memoir in Collaboration with Sue Dwiggins Worsley,* edited by Charles Ziarko. 1997
54. *Thorold Dickinson and the British Cinema,* by Jeffrey Richards. 1997
55. *The Films of Oliver Stone,* edited by Don Kunz. 1997
56. *Before, In and After Hollywood: The Autobiography of Joseph E. Henabery,* edited by Anthony Slide. 1997
57. *Ravished Armenia and the Story of Aurora Mardiganian,* compiled by Anthony Slide. 1997
58. *Smile When the Raindrops Fall,* by Brian Anthony and Andy Edmonds. 1998
59. *Joseph H. Lewis: Overview, Interview, and Filmography,* by Francis M. Nevins. 1998
60. *September Song: An Intimate Biography of Walter Huston,* by John Weld. 1998
61. *Wife of the Life of the Party,* by Lita Grey Chaplin and Jeffrey Vance. 1998
62. *Down But Not Quite Out in Hollow-weird: A Documentary in Letters of Eric Knight,* by Geoff Gehman. 1998
63. *On Actors and Acting: Essays by Alexander Knox,* edited by Anthony Slide. 1998
64. *Back Lot: Growing Up with the Movies,* by Maurice Rapf. 1999
65. *Mr. Bernds Goes to Hollywood: My Early Life and Career in Sound Recording at Columbia with Frank Capra and Others,* by Edward Bernds. 1999
66. *Hugo Friedhofer: The Best Years of His Life: A Hollywood Master of Music for the Movies,* edited by Linda Danly. 1999

67. *Actors on Red Alert: Career Interviews with Five Actors and Actresses Affected by the Blacklist,* by Anthony Slide. 1999
68. *My Only Great Passion: The Life and Films of Carl Th. Dreyer,* by Jean Drum and Dale D. Drum. 1999
69. *Ready When You Are, Mr. Coppola, Mr. Spielberg, Mr. Crowe,* by Jerry Ziesmer. 1999
70. *Order in the Universe: The Films of John Carpenter,* 2nd ed., by Robert C. Cumbow. 2000
71. *Making Music with Charlie Chaplin,* by Eric James. 2000
72. *An Open Window: The Cinema of Víctor Erice,* edited by Linda C. Ehrlich. 2000
73. *Satyajit Ray: In Search of the Modern,* by Suranjan Ganguly. 2000
74. *Voices from the Set: The Film Heritage Interviews,* edited by Tony Macklin and Nick Pici. 2000
75. *Paul Landres: A Director's Stories,* by Francis M. Nevins. 2000
76. *No Film in My Camera,* by Bill Gibson. 2000
77. *Saved from Oblivion: An Autobiography,* by Bernard Vorhaus. 2000
78. *Wolf Man's Maker: Memoir of a Hollywood Writer,* by Curt Siodmak. 2001
79. *An Actor, and a Rare One: Peter Cushing as Sherlock Holmes,* by Tony Earnshaw. 2001
80. *Picture Perfect,* by Herbert L. Strock. 2000
81. *Peter Greenaway's Postmodern/Poststructuralist Cinema,* edited by Paula Willoquet-Maricondi and Mary Alemany Galway. 2001
82. *Member of the Crew,* by Winfrid Kay Thackrey. 2001
83. *Barefoot on Barbed Wire,* by Jimmy Starr. 2001
84. *Henry Hathaway: A Directors Guild of America Oral History,* edited and annotated by Rudy Behlmer. 2001
85. *The Divine Comic: The Cinema of Roberto Benigni,* by Carlo Celli. 2001
86. *With or Without a Song: A Memoir,* by Edward Eliscu. 2001
87. *Stuart Erwin: The Invisible Actor,* by Judy Cornes. 2001
88. *Some Cutting Remarks: Seventy Years a Film Editor,* by Ralph E. Winters. 2001
89. *Confessions of a Hollywood Director,* by Richard L. Bare. 2001
90. *Peckinpah's Women: A Reappraisal of the Portrayal of Women in the Period Westerns of Sam Peckinpah,* by Bill Mesce Jr. 2001
91. *Budd Schulberg: A Bio-Bibliography,* by Nicholas Beck. 2001

92. *Between the Bullets: The Spiritual Cinema of John Woo*, by Michael Bliss. 2002
93. *The Hollywood I Knew: 1916–1988*, by Herbert Coleman. 2002
94. *The Films of Steven Spielberg*, edited by Charles L. P. Silet. 2002
95. *Hitchcock and the Making of Marnie*, by Tony Lee Moral. 2002
96. *White Horse, Black Hat: A Quarter Century on Hollywood's Poverty Row*, by C. Jack Lewis. 2002
97. *Worms in the Winecup: A Memoir*, by John Bright. 2002
98. *Straight from the Horse's Mouth: Ronald Neame, An Autobiography*, by Ronald Neame. 2003
99. *Reach for the Top: The Turbulent Life of Laurence Harvey*, by Anne Sinai. 2003
100. *Jackie Coogan: The World's Boy King: A Biography of Hollywood's Legendary Child Star*, by Diana Serra Cary. 2003
101. *Rungs on a Ladder: Hammer Films Seen through a Soft Gauze*, by Christopher Neame. 2003

Rungs on a Ladder

Hammer Films Seen through a Soft Gauze

Christopher Neame

Filmmakers Series, No. 101

The Scarecrow Press, Inc.
Lanham, Maryland, and Oxford
2003

SCARECROW PRESS, INC.

Published in the United States of America
by Scarecrow Press, Inc.
A Member of the Rowman & Littlefield Publishing Group
4501 Forbes Boulevard, Suite 200, Lanham, Maryland 20706
www.scarecrowpress.com

PO Box 317
Oxford
OX2 9RU, UK

Copyright © 2003 by Christopher Neame

All rights reserved. No part of this publication may be reproduced, stored
in a retrieval system, or transmitted in any form or by any means, electronic,
mechanical, photocopying, recording, or otherwise, without the prior permission
of the publisher.

British Library Cataloguing in Publication Information Available

Library of Congress Cataloging-in-Publication Data

Neame, Christopher, 1942–
   Rungs on a ladder : Hammer Films seen through a soft gauze / Christopher
Neame.
     p. cm.—(Filmmakers series; no. 101)
  Includes index.
  ISBN 0-8108-4735-3 (Hardcover : alk. paper)
  1. Hammer Film Productions. I. Title. II. Series.
  PN1999.H3 N43 2003
  791.43'651—dc21   2002156725

∞™ The paper used in this publication meets the minimum requirements of
American National Standard for Information Sciences—Permanence of Paper
for Printed Library Materials, ANSI/NISO Z39.48-1992.
Manufactured in the United States of America

Contents

Foreword by Christopher Lee		x
Principal Characters		xi
1	What Else?	1
2	String and Sealing Wax	9
3	The Next Rung	21
4	Wow!	33
5	BD	45
6	No Cowboys!	55
7	Egg and Chips	67
8	Brainless	85
9	Razor Blades and a Hand	95
10	Bludlust	105
11	Lengthening Shadows	113
Afterword		121
Appendix: Christopher Neame's Films with Hammer		125
Index		127
About the Author		131

Foreword

I have read *Rungs on a Ladder* with an element of nostalgia. So many happy memories of the Hammer days—so many recollections of outstanding casts and crews, working together in an atmosphere of mutual friendship and appreciation.

Christopher Neame's memoirs of his time as a technician are an object lesson to all those who wish to forge a permanent career in the film industry. Dedication, hard work, and professionalism: They apply to both sides of the camera. I well remember him leaping about in an apparent state of perpetual motion. The important thing is that he was never too proud to learn—a quality sadly missing in too many of my colleagues today, who think they know it all after one film.

Although the quality of Hammer productions declined over the years (and I should know), we both have the satisfaction of belonging to the most successful independent production company in the history of British film, a source of pride to us all.

—Christopher Lee

Principal Characters

(in order of appearance)

Michael (Mike) Reed:	Cinematographer
Anthony Nelson Keys (ANK):	Producer
Terrence (Terry) Fisher:	Director
Christopher Lee:	Actor
Les Bowie:	Special effects supervisor
Bernard (Bernie) Robinson:	Set designer
Arthur Grant:	Cinematographer
Moray Grant:	Camera operator, subsequently cinematographer (unrelated to Arthur Grant)
Don Sharp:	Director
John Gilling:	Director
Rosemary (Rosie) Burrows:	Wardrobe mistress
Eddie Powell:	Stuntman and Rosemary Burrows' husband
Irene Lamb:	Casting director
Roy Ashton:	Makeup artist
James Carreras ("The Colonel"):	Head of Hammer
Anthony Hinds:	Producer and writer ("John Elder") and son of Will Hinds ("Will Hammer")
Michael Carreras:	Producer, writer, and director and son of James Carreras
Kay Walsh:	Actress
Andrew Keir:	Actor
Michael Ripper:	Actor
Peter Cushing:	Actor

Principal Characters

Barbara Shelley:	*Actress*
Bette Davis:	*Actress*
Joan Fontaine:	*Actress*
Nigel (Tom) Kneale:	*Writer*
"Bluey" Hill:	*Assistant director*
Catherine Lacey:	*Actress*
Roy Ward Baker:	*Director*
Bert Batt:	*Assistant director and writer*
Jimmy Sangster:	*Writer, producer, and director*
Harry Waxman:	*Cinematographer*
Joan Harrison (Ambler):	*Producer*
Jack Fleischmann:	*Associate of Joan Harrison*
Norman Lloyd:	*Actor and producer*
Joseph (Joe) Cotton:	*Actor*
Roy Skeggs:	*Accountant, subsequently producer*
Don Chaffey:	*Director*
Tony Tenser:	*Executive producer (not part of Hammer)*
Seth Holt:	*Director*
Sally (Sal) Holt:	*Seth Holt's wife*
Oswald (Ossie) Haffenrichter:	*Seth Holt's editor*
Reg Varney:	*Comedian*
Frank Godwin:	*Producer*
Michael Stringer:	*Set designer*
Peter Sykes:	*Director*
Vincent Winter:	*Assistant director*
Judy Geeson:	*Actress*
Ralph Bates:	*Actor*
Joan Collins:	*Actress*
James Needs:	*Editor*
Christopher Neame:	*Actor (not the author)*

• *1* •

What Else?

It was inevitable from the start. The only profession I could enter when I grew up was film. This was not simply going to be treading in my father's footsteps, but my grandparents' as well. In 1908, one of Britain's popular newspapers ran the first Most Beautiful Woman in the World competition. The winner, Ivy Close, married the society and fashion photographer who took the pictures of all the contenders, Elwin Neame. Cinema was becoming a commercial operation by then, and an inventive photographer like Neame saw filmmaking as a challenge worth addressing. Together with his bride he made several films, but ultimately he preferred his work in a stills studio. In the meantime Ivy pursued her acting career with considerable success for some time, even spending a year working for a movie company in Florida.

Tragically, Elwin was killed in an automobile accident when my father was just thirteen, and before long the family's money began to run out. Unfortunately my grandfather did not believe in insurance, and by then Ivy was in her thirties and being offered fewer and fewer parts. The outcome was that after two years my father had to take on the role of breadwinner.

Ronald Neame started as a junior camera assistant at BIP Studios in Elstree and quickly worked his way up to become a successful cinematographer. His partnership with David Lean came about as a result of their second meeting on Noël Coward's *In Which We Serve*. (Noël was to become my godfather shortly thereafter.) Soon Ronnie became a producer and then a director. He has made a host of films, two of which—both starring Alec Guinness—are outstanding: *The Horse's Mouth* and *Tunes of Glory*. Other extremely good films followed, including *The Prime of Miss Jean Brodie*, with Maggie Smith, all leading up to his most financially successful movie, *The Poseidon Adventure*. He continued active work until he was in his mid-seventies, when at last we had the wonderful opportunity of doing something together—with him as director and me as producer. This was a small film called *Foreign Body*, starring the Indian actor, Victor Banerjee.

Throughout my childhood, actors, screenwriters, producers, cameramen, set designers, and more, had been a part of my everyday life. (My biggest chance of basking in another's glory was when I taught Gregory Peck how to play cricket—although I can't think why; it is a very tedious game.) Another factor influencing my decision to go into films was that we lived in the country, near Pinewood Studios, where my father was based. While I was growing up, this large and splendid lot became a second playground, and I was always made to feel welcome on anyone's set. Michael Powell allowed me to watch him film the sinking of the *Graf Spee* for *The Battle of the River Plate*. Then there were Bob Hope and Katharine Hepburn in *The Iron Petticoat*, Dirk Bogarde as Sydney Carton in *A Tale of Two Cities*, and Peter Finch in *Robbery under Arms*. Norman Wisdom was always good for a laugh as he clowned around both off camera as well as on.

My father, Ronnie, as I called him by then, counseled me, rather half-heartedly, I thought, against going into an industry that could offer no stability of employment. But I was determined, and so, when the time came, just before my eighteenth birthday, he spoke to Julian Wintle, a producer colleague, about a job for me at the old Beaconsfield Studios, which he was running with Leslie Parkyn under the banner of Independent Artists.

I started there in September 1960, at slightly below the bottom rung of the ladder, as a supernumerary with the job title of assistant camera maintenance engineer. A fat chance anyone ever had of getting a faulty movie camera working if it were only me around. That it had a set of lenses and was supposed to run at a film transportation speed of twenty-four frames per second was about the extent of my knowledge. After a year under the supervision of a chirpy man named Norman (Nobby) Godden, I was given the all-essential ACT union card and could graduate to the studio floor as a clapper boy. By late 1963 I had completed a wonderful three years of apprenticeship.

Probably the best-remembered film to have come out of the stable was Lindsay Anderson's *This Sporting Life*, starring the unforgettable Richard Harris and the gifted Rachel Roberts. Others included *The Wrong Arm of the Law*, a vehicle for Peter Sellers, and *The Fast Lady*. A lot of comedies were made at the studio, which was a delightful playground for some of the top British comedy actors of the day: Stanley Baxter, Leslie Phillips, and the irreplaceable James Robertson Justice. Julie Christie, who is much the same age as I am, made her screen debut there in *Crooks Anonymous*.

The duties of my humble role were to ensure that the film magazines were loaded and that the exposed film was dispatched each evening to the laboratories for overnight processing and to "click" the sticks (the clapper board) at the beginning of each shot, thereby giving the editors the wherewithal to synchronize the separate picture and sound track. (An old gag played on an unsuspecting new boy was to nail the clappers together.) Also, at least three times a day, I had to fetch tea and rolls for the camera crew, and woe betide a lad who served his department after another.

In the autumn of 1963 the studio closed (before reopening as the National Film School), and suddenly I found myself in the cold of the freelance world. Actually the timing worked out very well; my parents were about to sell our home and relocate to Italy, where they were having a house built. During the period before its completion Ronnie was going off to direct a film in Africa, and, after he discussed the possibility with the director of photography, I was given the opportunity of joining the unit. This was a big Hollywood-style movie starring Robert Mitchum, who was magical to work with. After some three months in Kenya, I was then fortunate enough to get another location assignment—this time in Southern Italy with Dirk Bogarde on *The High Bright Sun*.

By then I was ready to move on (or rather sideways). With the help of another introduction by my father, I secured a job as a junior agent with London Management. Nepotism it may be considered to have been, but my father's name went only as far as the entrée; after that I'd be on my own. In the end, working in an office in the West End of London wasn't for me, simply because the smell of a sound stage with its huge painted backings had become an essential "fix" in my life. I urgently needed to get back into the camera department to run for the tea and wield a clapper board again.

It is said that memories in the film industry are short, but I was lucky. Cameraman Michael Reed, with whom I had worked at Beaconsfield, answered my distress call and invited me to join his crew at Bray Studios on Hammer Films' *Dracula—Prince of Darkness* and, immediately afterwards, *Rasputin—The Mad Monk*. I was very excited and would probably have worked for nothing, but, being a reasonably responsible person, I had to inquire what the weekly salary would be.

"Oh, we never ask about that," Mike told me. Apparently the company's management would pay what they could and handled financial arrangements unilaterally. The money was never a large amount, but invariably fair.

In those days, with tiny crews compared to those of today, even Hammer could stretch its resources and give scripts to all. This, in my view, is essential because it involves everyone in the production as a whole and is a very simple way to make a unit truly a unit. Two days after I was taken on, and two weeks before the assignment was scheduled to begin, a copy of the script and my "letter of engagement" arrived through the post. Immediate disappointment set in, not because of the amount of the salary they were going to pay but, of all things, because of the notepaper. Looking back on my first reaction, I am astonished at my haughty opinion of my future employer's trademark. It was an unsightly crimson swathe across the top of an A4 sheet of paper and the better part of three inches deep; "Hammer" was in large white lettering and "Film Productions Ltd." in smaller black ones beneath. Immediately I must say that over the years I was to become very fond of this initially garish image. The only ongoing problem was that readers often missed the white name and simply sent replies to the company's letters to the more clearly defined "Film Productions Ltd., Wardour Street." In a street liberally sprinkled with filmmakers and distributors, it is a testament to the then Royal Mail's awareness of their customers that (to my knowledge anyway) all the post got through.

A far greater disappointment overcame my first when I settled down to read the screenplay. It was ghastly—not the writing itself, but the content: a man's throat slashed as he is suspended upside down, his blood pouring into Dracula's open grave; suggestive, semi-lesbian-type scenes that would most likely be devoid of the tension they should have; and a denouement, with Dracula dropping through cracking ice to his fate, that, unless filmed expensively, was destined to fall as flat as my heart had fallen by the time I had read the last page.

That evening Heather, my future wife, came around to my little cottage.

"I can't work on this film," I bleated.

"Why not? You wanted to get back to the studios."

"Yes."

"You shouldn't be complaining then."

"But this is worse than second feature rubbish." I had done some of those in the less high-profile days of Beaconsfield. But since then I had assisted the likes of the reigning kings of cinematography, Oswald Morris and Geoffrey Unsworth; been on exotic locations with director Ralph Thomas (a leader with the Rank Organization at Pinewood); and worked with Laurence Olivier and Maggie Smith on *Othello*. Even in my short number of months as an agent I had conversed and met with the doyens of the 1960s film industry.

I'm not sure Heather was overpersuasive, but it had to be accepted that there was no other immediate door open for a sort of returning minstrel. Well, *Dracula* it would have to be until I was reestablished.

Bray Studios at eight o'clock on a Friday morning for my one day of pre-production work—teeth gritted. Old familiar cameras, older than the ones at Beaconsfield; no proper camera department; one "third-world" camera dolly (lovingly cared for by Albert Cowlard, the grip); sets crammed into too little space (including the dining room of the old house, around which the studio existed, with its collapsing roof); and a fraction of Dracula's castle built on a small patch of adjacent land.

Within half an hour of my arrival at this sorry little studio Mike Reed, arrived. The warm smile on the face of this tall and genuinely kind-hearted man was welcoming and went a long way toward cheering me up. Quickly he, the senior camera assistant, Mike Rutter, and I got down to the business of preparing our equipment in a professional manner—and I started hearing some of the industry language that had been missing from my life. *Viewfinder, blimp, velocilator, basher, yashmak*. Mike, the other assistant, with whom I had also worked before, was particularly adept at using cockney rhyming slang. An amusing reference in this context is the Bristol bar. *Bristol* is short for Bristol City, which rhymes with titty, and this piece of inexpensive equipment would be positioned in front of a lamp so as to throw a shadow across a woman's chest, thereby emphasizing her attributes.

Around about eleven o'clock I was introduced to the film's producer, Anthony Nelson Keys. He was a small man with reddish hair turning to grey, a dark blue suit, and highly polished shoes. In a way he seemed a bit like a sergeant major, which made me think I'd better watch myself around him, or I'd be in big trouble. After he had scrutinized me for a second, which seemed like thirty, he said, "I worked as your father's clapper boy." This could have been good or bad news. If Ronnie had given him a hard time (which he might have, if deserved), the debt would probably be repaid; I had experienced such a thing before. But, on the other hand, maybe he'd be friendly. However, ANK, as I soon learned he was referred to, didn't seem overly so on our first meeting. So I called him "sir" for good measure. This was not simply a security measure of giving due respect to one's elders, but should be a matter of course for the junior members of a crew.

Bray Studios again, at seven-thirty the following Monday morning. Wheeling out the camera, setting it up, running it for ten minutes to get the oil flowing, lacing up the film, checking the parallax adjustment (this was for the viewfinder, which was about six inches to the side of the lens and consequently needed to be positioned in such a way as to allow the operator to see near enough what was actually being filmed through the camera lens). Then off to get the tea and cheese rolls. There I was, back where I wanted to be and determined to put all doubts behind me.

The director, Terence Fisher, arrived on the set, lit a cigarette, took a peg at a chipped, studio-sized cup of dark brown tea, and then, for no evident reason, laughed. It was an instantly engaging laugh starting somewhere in his belly and working its way up via his lungs to his throat to produce a chuckling wheeze as it spread to his eyes and often produced tears. The only problem for me was the bespectacled Terry didn't look like any of the film directors I had ever met in my life. I suppose it could be summed up by saying he had a bit of a paunch emphasized by the lateral tightness of a dark blue cardigan with an overly long downward trend and cigarette burn marks, a spotted cravat, and rather baggy blue trousers ending rather too far down over incongruous, weather-worn brown shoes.

Soon we were preparing the first setup—a tracking shot, under the "management" of Albert, moving to the outer limit of the set, which was about a foot from the so-called stage wall. Terry Fisher's laughter, it transpired, came about because the script called for a wide shot of the entrance hall of Dracula's castle. And such a shot was impossible, even though we were using Techniscope (a poor man's wide screen system created by the film stock's two-perforation pull-down, as opposed to the normal four).

By nine fifteen we were ready to shoot the Count descending the steps and looking out across the mountains toward his hoped-for guests. Albert nudged me. This affable, large man was grinning. "Dad-Drac is among us," he said as he nodded towards the stage door. I gasped—Christopher Lee looked nothing short of magnificent. His costume—the robe and his shirt, his well-fitting trousers, boots and other accoutrements—were visually rich beyond belief. The pearly fangs he could slowly reveal beneath his upper lip were both enticing and devastating. But it was his eyes that transfixed: dark, indeed piercing black, surrounded by no white at all, but deep blood red.

At that instant I realized that this apparently clumsy little film company had got all of its values right, and from then on I started to learn the real truth about filmmaking, both creatively and commercially.

Much has been written about Hammer Films, and most of it is pretty good stuff, so there is little purpose in my covering the same ground. What I will do here is look at seventeen productions, to a greater or lesser extent, from a personal point of view and do my best to describe the characters (many of whose names are still well-known) who ran or worked for this very special company.

· 2 ·

String and Sealing Wax

*S*een dimly through the mist swirling across the tomb are the decayed remains of a being. Then, as the fresh blood spurts down on it, veins begin to form, and slowly the body of the *undead* takes shape. Suddenly there's a sharp cut to a very close shot of Dracula's claw-like hand as it grabs the stone sides of what should have remained his final resting place. He rises.

Les Bowie, Hammer's regular mastermind when it came to complex optical work, created this visual effect. Les was not typecasting. He was a cross between a benign professor and a teddy bear, who would peer across the top of half-moon glasses with gentle, watery eyes. He had the wonderful ability of looking at an end situation and then taking it back to its simplest beginnings and rebuilding the structure in practical terms—invariably successfully. Dracula's reawakening for *Prince of Darkness* was done after the completion of principal photography by single frame shooting—animation, really. It remains, even today when computers can produce just about any combination of images, one of the most spectacular cinematic effects I have ever seen.

This was the stuff Hammer was made of—the ingenuity of a dedicated team made up of people like designer Bernard Robinson and his construction manager Arthur Banks; of cameramen Mike Reed and Arthur Grant, and Moray Grant (no relation) the camera operator; directors such as Terry Fisher, Don Sharp, and John Gilling; wardrobe mistress Rosemary Burrows and her husband, stunt man Eddie Powell; casting director Irene Lamb, makeup artist Roy Ashton, not to forget producer Anthony Nelson Keys and Pauline Harlow (née Wise). These are just a few of the people who pulled together to produce first-rate work for the least possible cost.

Chapter 2

By the time I arrived at the studio, the company was headed by Colonel (later Sir) James Carreras, Anthony Hinds (who wrote screenplays under the name of John Elder), and Michael Carreras (who, amusingly, called himself Henry Younger on the front of scripts). Another company director, involved with the sales and distribution side, was Brian Lawrence, not a sparkler like his partners but an erect and dapper man who certainly gave a fine impression of getting the job done.

As with any other business, the workforce of a film studio is only as good as those at the top, and these men were good. Had he wanted to, the Colonel could have sold Mars Bars to the Martians, such was his skill. It was rumored that all he had to do to convince the Hollywood majors to partly finance his pictures was to produce a poster with a scantily clad girl, bloody bite marks on her neck, stretched provocatively across an altar. This would be used as the cover for a script that wasn't even written—just so many pages of whatever. In 1967 we made *The Devil Rides Out,* and someone said the American partner's executives thought it was a Western because they hadn't bothered to read the script even when it had eventually been written. They must have had quite a shock when they saw the completed picture (if they saw it; perhaps they never bothered to run it but just sent it out to an avid audience). The Colonel also had a great eye for casting pretty actresses from around Europe. Some could sort of act, some not too well, and some not at all. But it didn't matter so long as they looked alluring and could scream well.

His son, Michael, could not compete with his father as a showman, but he was a good working producer nevertheless and a perfectly acceptable writer, although his talents as a director were less abundant. When I first met him, his hair was already turning to a fine silver and his moustache was quickly following suit. He was a man with a ready smile for those he respected, and teeth that could give painful bites to the unfortunate ones he did not—something I would witness a few years later during the filming of *Blood from the Mummy's Tomb.* The difference between Michael and the other executives of the company was that, while they were content to continue producing their brand of movies, Michael looked to more adventurous work, and sometimes this would bring about a division within the group.

Anthony Hinds is a charming man with distaste for confrontation. Probably what made him a good producer was the fact that he was not hands-on. In fact, he could willingly be entirely hands-off if he saw a difficulty arising. It may be apocryphal, but one story goes that when a certain film was running over schedule and therefore over budget, he did not arrive at the studio. Instead, he sent a telegram to the director and production manager informing them that they had to finish within two weeks, come what may. During this period, he went on to advise them, he would be abroad and out of contact. It has further been rumored that mischief-making senior personnel would stage an on-set row as a device for getting him out of the way—apparently it worked. As a writer, he was probably marginally better than Michael in terms of construction but could be accused of being unadventurous. The same characters would keep reappearing in similar situations, and the names of people and places infrequently varied. But that was unimportant, because the audience lapped up the fare he offered. When he was based at Bray, he would join the unit bus that left from Hammersmith and travel with the crew to work, everyone having breakfast together en route. Such a simple thing to do. And it is an example of why Hammer was a family—a happy family.

Many elements contributed to the unity, but the most important one was the complete faith and trust we had in our employers. They were all 100 percent fair and honest to a fault. My snobbish appraisal of the operation before I got to know it was completely out of order, and I can truthfully say I'd have been delighted to spend my entire career making films in that environment. Much later on, as a producer, I was to work with Euston Films (a subsidiary of Thames Television) and for a while re-tasted the atmosphere of my Hammer days.

Anthony Nelson Keys had obviously not suffered any maltreatment as my father's clapper boy and could not have been more kindly—firm, yes, but like everyone else, entirely fair. "Sir," as I continued to call him for some time, was part of an entertainment industry family. His father had been a music-hall comedian known as "Bunch Keys," and his elder brother was the director John Paddy Carstairs. His other brothers were production manager Basil Keys and editor Roddy. Years later, in a moment that would recall his father's career, I asked him to appear in a television series made by Hammer for Twentieth Century Fox called *Journey to the Unknown*. He was costumed and extravagantly made up to work alongside actress Kay Walsh as a burlesque performer.

Among many others important to me, there are three key people who helped me climb the rungs of my ladder: my father; a warm-hearted Scotsman called Bob McNaught (a sort of second father); and Mr. Keys.

Chapter 2

When ANK died in 1985, I wrote an obituary for an industry journal, assuming it would be used with many other pieces. It wasn't published, because the editor must have thought it too short. "He loved and was loved" said everything about him, without wearying the reader with a filmography. I owe him so much and will ever thank him for the many opportunities he gave me.

Books by filmmakers about the productions they have worked on have the terrible tendency to say "And then I did so and so"—the list simply getting longer and longer as they or the book goes on. This book is about Hammer, not about me. However, in this telling of some Hammer years I trust I may be forgiven for including my own learning experiences and describing my relationships with others along the way.

There it was again, Terry's infectious chuckle. This time it was caused by the splashing sound of blood pouring from the slashed neck of the victim suspended upside down over Dracula's tomb. The vivid red of Kensington Gore (an essential concoction for any horror movie) made it all the worse. Initially I was shocked at laughter over such a situation. But again, how wrong could I be? Soon I was to discover that this kindly man had long ago taken the view that the whole business had to be handled like a fantasy. There had to be laughter to avoid heavy-handedness—rather like the medics' behavior in M*A*S*H. Had Terry not taken this approach, the movies would have become leaden and plain nasty. The laughter (unheard by the audience) behind the camera had the effect of taking the weight off the horror scenes, and, to the initiated, it shows in the finished film.

During the fifties and sixties, many producers and directors would tend to gather around them "stock players"—in Hammer's case, for example, Andrew Keir or Thorley Walters, or Michael Ripper, not to mention Christopher Lee and Peter Cushing. This wasn't because of a lack of imagination or idleness on their part, although it might seem so in retrospect; it actually had to do with security. Working to very tight schedules made it essential to have actors who were reliable in every respect. Therefore "better the devil you know" (not that any were devils), or, to use an industry adage, "actors who knew all their jokes and wouldn't bump into the furniture."

At Bray everything conceivable was done to ensure a smoothly running production, and experimentation was rare—it usually went wrong! This seemingly mundane approach carried on through to the editing and music-recording stages as well. Music recording is a very expensive procedure, with musicians charging a small fortune for a three-hour session. Moreover, before the days of sophisticated keyboards, it wasn't until the first session that the producers knew whether the music was any good or not. Such was the power of the Musicians Union that it was not unknown for the players to lay down their instruments halfway through the recording of a track at the instant the second hand on the studio clock clicked over the line. Pursuant to the policy of "playing safe," Hammer almost always engaged the same composers. The musical director was Philip Martell, a small and lively man vaguely reminiscent of a sparrow. I confess to being unaware of exactly what he did at first but was later to discover his tremendous ability as a conductor. Always an important role, the conductor's task becomes exacting in the finest sense when the orchestra more often than not has to finish a section bang on a cut—and with various moments throughout, say a two-minute piece, having to hit a particular cue within a twenty-fourth of a second. For *Prince of Darkness* the score was written by a regular, James Bernard, and a good score it is, too. What a joy for composers these types of films were. They could pull all their old tricks out of the bag and were never in danger of going over the top. O.T.T is the usual way of expressing the occurrence; however, in Hammer's case R.O.T.B.T. was also thoroughly acceptable—Right Over The Bloody Top! Who cares? It worked.

Memories of my first film at Bray are vague, although I still carry the tiniest evidence of one minor mishap. So pleased was I to be back on a sound stage that I was a little overeager when nailing down a crow's foot. These are small blocks of wood with a "V" cut into them, used to stop tripod legs from sliding apart under the weight of the camera. I hit my own nail—not the one I was aiming for!

Another (painless) recollection, although still misty, was of a growing awareness of the ingenuity and unique ability of Bernard Robinson, the production designer, in his work on *Dracula*. My appreciation of his work became fully focused with the second production, *Rasputin*, which was directed by Don Sharp. The two films were made back-to-back— one finished on the Friday evening at exactly five-twenty and the other started at eight-thirty on the next Monday morning. *Dracula* was a large-scale production made on the floor space of so many postage stamps and *Rasputin*, with settings in the Winter Palace at St. Petersburg, called for even more production values. But the art department only had a weekend to convert Transylvanian interiors into Russian. This was where Bernie came into his own. Time was not the only limitation. In the early 1960s, Bray studios, which lies on the south bank of the River Thames not far from the lovely town of Windsor, consisted of four so-called sound stages. The largest was about the size of a small to medium stage at Pinewood. (It was destroyed by fire a few years later.) The second was some sort of converted workshop and was small. The third (a proper stage) was very, very small indeed. And the previously mentioned dining room of the old house made up the fourth.

A quiet person of mild temperament, Bernie looked like an artist from his brown suede shoes to the top of his wispy head. During World War II he had been engaged in creating dummy airfields across southern England. They were put down to give the Germans a tempting target—they were not made too easy to attack, but they weren't so difficult either. This work must have contributed to the clever way in which he designed and built his sets. By taking out the (mock) stone stairs leading a short way up from Dracula's castle's entrance hall and repositioning them the other way round, he began the transformation. The side walls were swivelled round, the bleak stonework now hidden as previously prepared gilt and pastel colors were revealed. A couple of panels were removed and now there were palace windows, with a well-painted canvas backing beyond. Imitation marble flooring made of paper was laid over Dracula's painted grey flagstones. The sound of footsteps on marble would be added later. Given lush dressing here and there, and we had the full glory of the Romanoff home. Finally, with several of the *Dracula* actors (Francis Matthews, Barbara Shelley, and Suzan Farmer) recostumed, we were up and away for a good film, though not at the cutting edge of historical facts!

Another set was a large café, which was built in the converted workshop with its sides standing about six inches from the "stage" walls. Of course, such a thing would be illegal today, and it probably was then, but so what? The first setup completed, we repositioned the camera and asked the large sound recordist to find a place "out of shot" for himself and his equally bulky recording desk. Ken Rawkins, known as "Rhino" because he looked a bit like one, complied rather grudgingly. When it came to the next setup, the same request was made. Grumpily he started the move, but discovered that a scenery flat had been nailed down over one of his cables, trapping him. He was getting really rattled by the time it was released and he was settled into a new position. The fourth shot was one too many for him and he refused point-blank to move again. The more we insisted, the more he dug his heels in. The impasse was finally overcome by quickly erecting a piece of scenery around Rhino!

Another problem at Bray was the electricity. A lot of lights were needed for this café sequence—too many, in fact, for the system to cope with. The electrical breakers kept tripping and mucking up takes. Eventually the Best Boy (the second senior electrician) took the matter into his own hands and, with a bit of sash cord, tied the breakers up in their "on" position. Of course this was a definite no-no in health and safety terms, particularly since the set half-covered the door, precluding a quick exit by anyone in case of fire. But no one let such a small thing be of concern. We had a film to make, and it was the most important thing in the world for us, from the director right down to the clapper boy.

The fire risk was greater still for a scene that took place in a barn. The set was put up in the old dining-room stage. Straw was scattered liberally around, and the action called for one of the characters to overturn an oil lamp, thereby starting a fire. It's hardly believable that we could have done that.

Production wasn't confined to the studio sets. Black Park, so called because it resembled (in someone's mind) the Black Forest in Germany, was a location used regularly by many companies. Located directly alongside Pinewood Studios, parts of it were used as the surroundings of a Malaysian village, a Japanese prisoner-of-war camp, Sherwood Forest, and plenty of other places, including Transylvania, naturally. This time it was the Russian countryside, with Rasputin traveling to the capital.

Christopher Lee, out of his black and scarlet cloak, his red eyes and fangs removed, was now the bearded mad monk. Unlike that of the vampire, this role gave him plenty of lines of dialogue and he delivered them all impeccably. But here we faced an ongoing problem for filmmakers. If a story is set in a non-English-speaking country, what language should the characters speak? Well, obviously, in a bit of British cinema, they had to speak our language, but with or without a Russian accent, in this instance? One theory—and it's a very sound one—is that a character should have a hint of an accent in the first few moments on screen, slowly giving way to a dialect-free voice. Christopher succeeded in this by giving us a little inconsequential Russian dialogue before "segueing" into his natural voice. I think his ability as a singer helped him to make a seamless switch between the two. Probably his portrayal of the self-proclaimed mystic is one of his finest performances from that period. Sad to say, the film is now little remembered, but it is worth watching on television when the opportunity arises.

Mr. Keys was the producer again, and I found a couple of occasions to talk to him about the overall operation. Like most people asked about the intricacies of their profession, he was a willing informer. At this time I had not focused on any goal within the industry (more concerned with becoming an acceptably professional clapper boy) and was, therefore, a careful listener. One question I recall asking him was what protection a production might have if bad weather precludes shooting. Was there an insurance policy to cover inclemency? He explained in some detail why the cost of insurance was prohibitive and how the schedule should allow for alternative ways to continue shooting. What happened, and indeed still happens, is something called "weather cover," whereby a full working day on interior sets is scheduled alongside the exterior "call"—wherever possible utilizing the same actors. True, there was traveling time back to the base and the time of resetting-up, but the cost of such was a smallish amount compared to the cost of a day that might otherwise be lost. Throughout my long career as a producer, the fairly drastic step of "calling the weather cover" has been necessary remarkably seldom. One situation (although, as it happens, far from anything to do with the weather) was dealt with in a similar manner when a tragedy befell Peter Cushing.... But this sad moment was yet to come.

I daresay Black Park resembles parts of Russia; Barbara Shelley gave a performance convincingly combining sophistication with earthy sexuality, and after six weeks *Rasputin* "wrapped" on schedule. Michael Reed and the rest of his camera team (including me) had finished our term with Hammer and said adieu to this funny little "lot" with some sadness.

We remained together on a film made in North Africa (*Our Man in Marrakesh* with Tony Randall), and during one of many phone calls from the location to Heather at home in England, we became engaged. I was just twenty-two years old. My family life will not occupy much space in these pages; I will refer to it only when there is either some relevancy to Hammer or the reader (like the writer) could do with a break from ongoing film production.

Harry Alan Towers, nicknamed "El Sombrero" because of his initials, was responsible for this African production, and we stayed with him to make a second picture, *Circus of Fear*, back at Bray. Christopher Lee was the star, and for all intents and purposes it was almost like a Hammer film, but not quite. For some reason it lacked the unique quality of the latter's work—probably because it was not sufficiently tongue-in-cheek.

Although not actually shooting at the time, Anthony Nelson Keys still maintained an office at the studio, and one day I had a long chat with him about my plans for the future. When first entering the industry, my father had insisted it should be in the camera department. This was good advice, as the camera is the essential tool, and by understanding how to use it properly one could gain an insight into the way movies are crafted. Particularly important is to learn how different lenses create different effects. The real bonus for a clapper boy (more properly referred to as the Clapper/Loader) is that he is probably the closest person to the actors throughout a take; having announced the shot number, he must simply duck out of frame and remain still. The art of clapping, if it can be called an art, is to reflect the mood of a scene. It's no good mumbling out, "Three-twenty-seven, take one" and softly tapping the sticks together for a long shot. You've got to be big. "THREE-TWENTY-SEVEN, TAKE ONE"—BANG! Should the scene be an intimate one, the announcement has to be soft; if it's supposed to be funny, some amusement in the voice is permissible. Another little trick was to blow any chalk residue off the board (the setup and take numbers were always chalked on at that time), so as to avoid scattering an actor's dark costume with white powder.

But as much as I loved the work, I wanted to do more in the creative field. Once someone has progressed from the bottom to the top in the camera department, there is ordinarily nowhere else for them to go. Very few cinematographers have become directors (my father being a notable exception, along with Nicolas Roeg and a clutch of others), and producers rarely come via such a route.

My initial plan was to move into the cutting rooms, because that is, or certainly was then, the perfect stepping-stone toward direction. People often ask what a director does. Although the practical side of the job requires considerable experience and energy, the definition is actually straightforward—he or she is a storyteller. That, of course is putting it very simply; there are many facets to the job: casting, picking suitable locations, approving set and costume designs, shooting within a given schedule. The editor is the assistant storyteller, with his or her concerns confined to that alone (other than to know how physically to handle film).

Mr. Keys told me that he would be willing to hire me as a junior in the cutting room on the next film he produced. Then I began thinking carefully about it. Did I really want to take that course? Doing so would be treading too much in the footsteps of my father. My own identity was essential if I were to survive, so I seriously started considering the production department.

Prehistoric Women, shot entirely on a stage at Elstree, was to be my last camera assignment, and it brought me promotion. This film was photographed in CinemaScope, an anamorphic process. The history of anamorphosis is fascinating. Thousands of years ago in China it was used for viewing pornography! A painted flat surface of what appeared to be random swirls would be laid on a table and a highly reflective cylinder placed at its center. By looking into it, the images became unsqueezed and the voyeur could satisfy his lust. For cinema, a special lens is fitted to the front of the camera lens to produce squeezed images on a standard thirty-five-millimeter frame. When projected, the beam passes back through another anamorphic lens to produce a very wide, undistorted picture on the screen. My job was to be the co-assistant cameraman. I would be on one side of the camera "pulling focus" on the attachment lens while my "oppo," Mike Roberts, kept the primary lens sharp. Mike would go on to become one of the most revered camera operators in the industry and was to die far too young.

Michael Carreras was the director of this rather silly film, which seems to have been made solely to cash in on the success (and costumes—what there were of them) of *One Million Years BC*. He had also written the script. The problem was that Michael didn't have quite good enough storytelling qualities, however spirited he was on the set.

When it was released, the title was changed in various markets to *Slave Girl,* and I cannot help commenting on how incredibly stupid this kind of thing is. Just give it a thought; is someone in Boise, Idaho, going to be naïve enough to assume that *Prehistoric Women* is a sexy romp featuring nonagenarians? More likely, rain-coated men in the Far East will think *Slave Girls* is a bondage flick. The right title has always been vexatious. Some will argue that it is a powerful draw for an audience, others that it is unimportant. In reality the pull is a good movie, and if the title is good, so much the better. Take a look at the filmography at the end of these pages and check out the ludicrous changes!

There was one advantage during the shooting of this one—a lot of pretty, bikini-clad girls, including the very sexy Martine Beswick. However I had to behave myself and concentrate on lenses, as marriage was not far off my horizon.

And now the moment had arrived when career decisions had to be made. ANK came to the rescue.

· 3 ·

The Next Rung

"Go away at once, you rude boy," yelled Kay Walsh.

Hastily I retreated from the actress's location caravan in some surprise. Having opted to join the production department, I was now a third assistant director on another film for Hammer—*The Witches,* starring Joan Fontaine—and one of my many tasks was to ensure the cast was "on set" when required, the byword being "the camera should never be kept waiting by anyone." Actors have a difficult time when it comes to hanging around, because, in order to be instantly available, they may be called to the studio or a location early in the morning, and end up not being used until much later in the day (or not at all, if it comes to weather cover or a tardy director). Yet they have to remain in a state of readiness, both in terms of costume and makeup (in the case of Hammer, frequently complicated) and at the correct emotional pitch to give a performance. Too few filmmakers make allowances for the problem; their position, very unfair to my mind, is "The bloody actors are being paid handsome money and deserve no sympathy." Nevertheless, the bottom line is that holdups of any sort are unacceptable. It is good to be able to record that most actors are highly responsible and arrive on time, or nearly on time. The only (reverse) exception to this, in my experience, was Bette Davis, who was never, never, ever anything but early to the set. I would work with this purportedly fearsome lady on *The Anniversary.*

So there was I doing my job and seeing that Kay Walsh was escorted to the camera on time and getting a heavy earful for my pains. The normal routine was a knock at her door, followed by a respectful wait, followed by a quiet entry. On every occasion, bar this one, she greeted me with, "Good morning, Kitty-kar." (Apparently, that was how she heard me say my name when I was very small and she was married to my father's then partner, David Lean.) On this occasion, however, she was dressed only in her underwear when I entered. Actresses dressed in such a state, or even less, are not unusual sights for third assistant directors, who, if gentlemanly, will politely avert their eyes from bare breasts. What panicked her was that I might have noticed that her corset was a Marks and Spencer's item and she didn't want me telling my mother, who, she wrongly thought, considered only Harrods corsets acceptable for ladies!

Joan Fontaine (the sister of the better remembered Olivia de Havilland) had owned the rights to the novel on which *The Witches* was based for some time and obviously saw the subject matter and the principal role as a vehicle for herself. She certainly gave a very professional performance, but she was overshadowed by Kay and must have known it, because Kay told me she was not very pleasant to her—actually rather unkind.

We had a good cast, including some of Hammer's regulars. Duncan Lamont was one of them. Also featured was the irresistible *grande dame*, Gwen Ffrangcon Davies. There was one problem with the magnificent Gwen—she had a squint and this made close-ups difficult to shoot. It is a hard-and-fast cinematic rule that if a character is talking to another who is off-screen, the eye-line must be maintained. In other words, if actor A, in close-up, is talking to someone on the right side of the camera, actor B must look to the left for his or her matching close-up so as to make it clear they are facing one another. Because of Gwen's squint, whatever we did, it always appeared that she was looking in the opposite direction from the one in which she actually was looking.

The Witches tells of a schoolmistress returning from Africa (where she had been involved in a contretemps with a witch doctor) and taking up a post at a small village school. Soon she discovers she is in the midst of a witches' coven and has to save a girl who is in danger of being sacrificed to the greater glory of Satan. Cyril Frankel did a journeyman job as director, but he could hardly go wrong, because the screenplay was written by the excellent Nigel (Tom) Kneale, whose many credits include the *Quatermass* films and series.

The first and second assistant directors were, dare I say it, outstanding at their jobs; however, I regret to say, the third assistant was not. It was a strange transition from clapper boy, where the work was second nature to me, to becoming a sort of callboy. I had to make a conscious effort not to take on my old role, but I really didn't know what my new one was or how to handle efficiently the various errands required of me. I usually got something wrong. It just seemed like a lot of running, and, in my case, running in ever-decreasing circles.

The location shooting was done at a very pretty flint and brick village called Hambledon, which is only a dozen or so miles from Bray, where the interiors were filmed. For one scene there, which took place in the schoolmistress's bedroom, Joan wore slightly see-through pajamas—brave for a woman of nearly fifty and at a time when even the vague shape of a nipple was a rarity on screen.

Arthur Grant was the cameraman. He was not among the top cinematographers in the country, but he wasn't half bad, and he was quick—and that was a critical factor. He was very much of the old school, in both his lighting style and attire. Arthur was a dear man, but his dress sense was a little below par when it came to his contemporaries at Bray—shiny suit with a tie and incongruous shirt, usually with a curly collar. (Not that any of them were exactly à la mode in this area, although Mr. Keys was always nattily presented.)

As for lighting style, Arthur would have a mixture of 2K and 5K lamps on a gantry. These are tungsten spotlights, which cast a harsh light and are useful for overall illumination as well as giving strong backlight. The trick was to avoid double shadows, this being a criminal offense in the eyes of the British Society of Cinematographers. Spots were also used for the foreground, usually the smaller type like a "pup," which could be repositioned quickly for different setups. The method was to light the long shot for atmosphere, then leave it in place for the close-ups, and individually light the leading ladies so they looked their best. Experienced screen actors will know exactly where their "key light" should be positioned and, if they have the clout, can insist that the cameraman light them as they, themselves, would wish. Nowadays the lighting is much softer, and the harsh lights on the gantry are very much a thing of earlier times.

Heather and I had married a few weeks before production commenced, and ANK, being most thoughtful about my tenuous ability as a breadwinner, kept me on the payroll between *The Witches* and the next picture, *Frankenstein Created Woman*. The two- or three-week gap between productions was necessary for preparation as, this time, the two films had nothing in common whatsoever—the former was a modern-day subject—and Bernie Robinson could not possibly schedule the two back-to-back. During this hiatus I became the entire production department, working like a runner (or gofer) when it came to copying scripts on an old Gestetner machine, and like a production manager when it came to paying a crew called in for the day to do makeup tests on our next female star, Susan Denberg. Also I doubled as the first assistant director for these tests. Really quite scary.

I'd seen enough first assistant directors at work and wasn't at all sure I would be able to emulate even the worst. The first assistant is the person who runs the set on behalf of the director, who should be concerning himself with the storytelling aspect. So there I was, all of twenty-three years old, and in charge of the "floor"—fair game for a gang of electricians and studio craftsmen. They all behaved very badly and chattered through a rehearsal Terry Fisher was taking with a stumbling Miss Denberg. How to react? Very quietly I called for silence and said as authoritatively as I possibly could, "Gentlemen, it is extremely bad manners and very thoughtless of you to distract a director and an actress when they are trying to concentrate. And you know it even better than me." There was absolute quiet from the shamefaced crew for the subsequent rehearsals and the take. I suspect this happened for two reasons: They knew it was wrong, and they felt sorry for a lad who had been dropped into the deep end. Anyway, it worked and taught me that a first assistant director doesn't have to shout to be heard. The bad ones invariably yell the loudest, "QUIET!" No need; there is enough stress on a film set as a unit strives for both speed and perfection.

This desire for perfection is another essential ingredient along with the belief that the film one is currently working on is the best film in the world. Even if one knows deep down that something is a bit second-rate, it is necessary to quash inner rebellion or it becomes impossible to carry on. Susan Denberg didn't help in this respect. There is a very enticing publicity shot of her, naked but for a peignoir clasped to her breast and on down her front. It's about all we get to see of her sexual attributes in connection with this film. Her spread in *Playboy* most likely revealed more. Many consider her to have done a good job in the role, but in my opinion, casting this girl was probably the biggest error the Colonel ever made. Never mind; the rest of the picture was at Hammer's gothic best with an interesting new angle—transplanting the soul of a young man, wrongly guillotined for a murder, into his girlfriend's body. The plot concerns his/her revenge.

The greatest joy for me was to work with Peter Cushing—just to think that this mildest of men could ever have played the cold-hearted Baron Frankenstein so convincingly! It was certainly a testament to his ability and sheer professionalism. Some actors, far too few, thoroughly research their parts and build a character by their individual methods. Alec Guinness, for example, seemed to start at the feet and work his way upward to the top of his head. How a character walked was something he needed to know from the outset. I don't know Peter's method for sure, but I suspect it was to do with his hand props. He was always most particular about selecting them for himself—perhaps his cane, perhaps his watch, the scalpel he would use when operating, the napkin at his table. Each script he worked on was meticulously broken down; his beautifully penned notes were about equal in number of words to the screenplay itself. Yet with all this intensity of work, he was relaxed and natural on screen—and off, as well. Somehow he always found time for everyone, and there was not a fraction of an ounce of superiority about him. God bless Peter Cushing for his kindness to me, particularly on one special occasion during a later film.

Someone else working on *Frankenstein Created Woman* taught me a great deal about being an assistant director, although by reverse example. Stan, who in his thirties must have seemed comparatively old by my standards, was the second assistant. Sad to say, Stan was inept. If something could be done incorrectly, Stan was your man. The first assistant was a rather boring, tall fellow who was the son of an earlier assistant director. The erect Doug Hermes had no "color" but could do his job efficiently enough. Why on earth he chose the clutching Stan as his aide is unfathomable.

Extras in those days were simply required to turn up for work to fill spaces. Should they be asked to do anything other than pick their noses, they demanded additional money—known as "special action" money. One of these people, possibly fairly, claimed a further payment for one scene, and Stan didn't concur. Stan won his case, but thirty extras went into overtime because their bus back to London was delayed half an hour by the argument. Here was a classic example of being penny-wise and pound-foolish. Taking note, I devised a scheme to make sure no such a situation would happen to me, which was to prove invaluable on *Quatermass and the Pit*.

The handling of extras requires tact and sensitivity. Like every other person in the world, they must be given dignity. Within just a few weeks

I was to treat five members of this very important team so unfairly that I still have self-disgust at my action. Again, I would learn from it. Frankly, Stan's incompetence opened doors of understanding for me, and I am sorry I cannot be kinder about his contribution to this film.

I was able to escape Stan's supervisory clutches one day when a rather curious thing happened. We were in Black Park filming a sequence in which the Susan Denberg character, "Christina" (a typical name selected by John Elder), runs toward a ravine and throws herself into the rushing waters far below. The ravine was off-camera, and the reverse shot would be filmed elsewhere—there are no ravines in Black Park. At around eleven o'clock, the first camera assistant, the focus-puller, was taken ill and had to leave. The clapper boy was fairly inexperienced and was not ready to take over, so I was asked to do so. What a terrific time—stepping back into the camera department for a few hours! Everything went very well, but if the truth were told, I wasn't focus-puller material. In confessing this, I usually add, "The job requires real skill, so I gave it up and became a producer instead."

A nice moment (one of several on Hammer Films) offered itself up when we had finished with a particularly gory prop. As requested, I was returning the head of the guillotined young man to the art department when I passed the open door to the canteen kitchen. "Annie," I said to one of the girls, "here, catch." And I tossed the head to her—she caught it and screamed. Little wonder I got a cool hot lunch that day. In hindsight it seems to have been a bit cruel, but we were all up to this kind of larking about.

After the completion of principal photography, one stunt shot remained to be done, the reverse angle of "Christina" jumping into the torrent in the ravine. For this we had to use a double, and, because of the power of the water, it had to be a man. Ideally the location should have been somewhere in northern Europe, but budgetary restrictions precluded that, so instead it was a weir on the River Thames, just a few miles away from Bray.

While the camera was being set up to look down on the water, I asked a couple of men to drag the weir to ensure that there were no hidden dangers beneath the surface. This took rather a long time and Moray

Grant, promoted for the day from camera operator to cameraman, became impatient to start shooting.

"Come on, let's go."

"Not until I'm certain it's safe," I told him rather curtly.

He strummed his fingers in evident boredom. Ten minutes later the men found an upward-pointing, sharp metal stake embedded in the mud at the bottom. Moray apologized at once. I mention this event not to prove how right I was but to illustrate Moray's drive. He was a terrific operator (and later director of photography, although oddly insecure), who had the ability to jockey a crew along. In a way he was an invaluable additional assistant director. No one ever had to wait for him.

Hammer productions have moved into the realm of the cult film, and I find this surprising. Nothing in its work could be considered examples of pioneering cinema. Rather, they were commercial products for the then audience and have now, somehow, found their way into the history books of film. So two questions come to mind: Why did they appeal to audiences of the fifties and sixties? And why is there so much interest in them some forty years on? To answer the first: Television was still unsophisticated, and the public knew they would get value for money from a Hammer film and in the bargain they could cower in fright under the seat and scream freely. It was a sort of early interactive experience. As for the longevity, it could be because of any number of things: well-crafted work, fond memories of the mid-twentieth century, or the charisma of the gothic stars. Who knows? Personally I am inclined to think it is nothing more than a fluke. True, the films were of a genre and therefore packageable as a recognizable entity, but as no one has yet been able to predict successes in a "gold mining" type of business, I'll stay with my own gut reaction. Still, an audience who enjoyed *Dracula* would doubtless want to see *Dracula—Prince of Darkness* and all the subsequent Draculas. It has to be as simple as that and no amount of analysis can prove otherwise.

"Bluey" was very drunk—drunker that night than on most nights, yet not so drunk as to realize that no self-respecting cabby would stop to pick him up and take him home in his condition. As a good first assistant director, he fought through the murk of his mind and engaged his brain. Hooking his arms around some railings bordering houses on a central London street, he managed to remain sort of upright and sort of steady. From this position, he hailed a taxi. The trouble was that it wasn't a taxi but a police car. Bluey spent the night in a cell at Savile Row police station. He was released at ten o'clock the following morning and ordered to appear before magistrates on a charge of being drunk and disorderly an hour later. Putting his professional duties before all else, he opted to duck this and rush out to Bray Studios, where I was standing in for him as first assistant director.

There are countless stories about this larger-than-life Australian, who by the time I met him was getting on in years. Nicknamed Bluey because at one time he had had flaming red hair, Bluey Hill was legendary among assistant directors. Once when a director needed to film London's Tower Bridge during the day without cars crossing it, it was Bluey who found a way of achieving the impossible. The lights that controlled traffic on the bridge allowed passage in one direction at a time. "The second there are no cars," he advised the crew, "roll the camera. You'll have thirty seconds to get the shot." With that he disappeared. Five minutes later the bridge was free of all vehicles. What this outrageous character had done was to lie down in the road in front of a car an instant before the lights turned green in its favor!

Arriving on location in India for one production, he was told it was a "dry" country. Without a word Bluey turned round and headed back to the aircraft. He was persuaded to get off the plane only when he was told that he could be registered as an alcoholic and get his needed fix.

The extras on the very low budget TV series he was doing there were each paid two handfuls of rice a day. Before selecting any of them, Bluey had to make sure he picked those with the smallest hands.

Now, on this particular day at Bray, it was time to play a trick on him. His failure to appear before the magistrates was bound to bring him problems, so I grabbed two of our extras and took them round to Rosie Burrows in the wardrobe department to be kitted out as policemen. When they returned to the set, I went over to Bluey and said they had come to see him. Without a word, he quickly left the stage by another door and I took over as first assistant for another half an hour. He was tremendously good-natured about it when he found out about the gag and laughed along with everyone else. I never knew the legal outcome for his double misdemeanour, but whatever it was, it didn't keep him from working or drinking.

Laughing on the set is an essential; it relieves those too frequent moments of tension. Doubtless it would not be encouraged today, and more's the pity. Bluey was the sort of person who would ask for silence on the stage prior to a take, wait until everyone was poised for action and then, of all things, tell a joke—and they weren't always short. However, his timing on one occasion was misjudged.

The film we were shooting was *The Mummy's Shroud*, written and directed by John Gilling from a story by Anthony Hinds. It took Gilling five days to complete the script. I know, because my job was to take each finished scene along to Pauline, Mr. Keys's secretary, for typing on "skins," and then run off the pages on the Gestetner machine. Certainly no great movie came from it, but it was fun to make, nonetheless—especially shooting desert sequences in some military-controlled sandpits a short distance south of Heathrow Airport in late autumn.

A sandstorm was required for these desert scenes, and Les Bowie and his team created one by running up large aircraft engines and hurling in vast quantities of fuller's earth. (Basically this is pretty harmless stuff, but on a later mummy film, it would contribute to the untimely death of the director.) These days, even a television movie would go on location to a real desert, but for Hammer such a luxury was only occasionally affordable and reserved for their higher-profile productions like *One Million Years BC*. It also happened to be fortunate that audiences weren't as discerning then and were certainly far less well traveled, so with a bit of imagination difficult sequences could be quite convincing. After all, Hammer had re-fought the battle of the Spanish Armada, or something similar, in the water-filled gravel pits at the back of Bray.

Our extras from Central Casting, for the Egyptian sequences back in the studio, were authentic enough and needed little or no makeup. Neither did actor Roger Delgado, who was of Spanish descent, but the fair-skinned Catherine Lacey (playing a dribbling Arab fortune-teller) most certainly did. (This venerated actress was, a few years later, to turn my first stumblings as a dialogue writer into a riveting scene, but more of that and how it came about later). In addition to Miss Lacey, there were several others who needed similar makeup treatment. Now here's what happened. In order to create a wide lighting contrast outside the windows of a darkened set, Arthur Grant, was using "brutes"—very large arc lights—and the temperature on the tiny stage rocketed. This could be overcome by leaving the stage door open wide until the moment to shoot arrived. And soon enough it did arrive.

"Close the doors," called Bluey. "Red light. Stand by!" And that's when he told one of his lengthy jokes. By the time he'd got to the punch line the actors' makeup had run in the heat and we had to start all over again. Still, it was a funny story and even John Gilling, not known for his patience, laughed at it.

It seems by now that Mr. Keys had had sufficient faith in my ability to promote me to second assistant director. It was either that or because I'd won a brownie point by solving a little problem for executive producer Anthony Hinds. Although it was at short notice, he desperately wanted to get away to the South of France for a long weekend break, but all the flights to Nice and Marseilles were full. Hearing of his plight, I offered the solution I had used in similar circumstances when visiting my parents in Italy via Nice.

"You could take a flight to Paris, change there and pick up an internal flight." He looked at me in astonishment. "I hadn't thought of that."

Five minutes later Air France confirmed his two-flight passage.

Being a second assistant is one of the truly great jobs in the film industry (if unnecessary paperwork can be avoided), the role being a kind of conduit between the shooting crew and the production office, and representing the latter's interest when away from the studio. Another responsibility is preparing the "call sheet" for the following day's work: estimating how long scenes would take to shoot and at what time the actors should be ready on set. The best days of all are when a large number of extras are on call. At first this is daunting, because the second assistant has to manage the entire affair (admittedly with the help of the third assistant), including the control of cost, but as I grew more experienced and my confidence increased, I enjoyed the task of positioning them and working out their moves and timing. It wasn't until an exciting production the following year that sufficient numbers were on call for me to get a real buzz and until then I had to make do with twenty at the most.

Bernie Robinson had cleverly and simply created an Arab market against one wall at Bray by covering it with brightly coloured fabrics; positioning stalls laden with pots and pans along its length, and, running parallel, various foreground objects. And Arthur Grant lit the whole with two brutes. A right-to-left camera tracking shot was designed to take the principals along the street, and my task, under Bluey and John Gilling's guidance, was to dress in the extras. A third of the way through the scene, the principals would stop to exchange some dialogue, while I rustled my team round behind the camera from one end to the middle of the market. Once quickly positioned, the track continued for another third of the distance and again there was a pause for chat—and again I relocated the extras to the far end. By the time it was all over, sixty Arabs appeared to be bustling around and as a result of twisting and turning them about, and changing a headdress or two, none of the actual twenty would be recognizable from one section to the next.

At exactly 5:00 P.M. the extras would click into overtime, so it was up to me to get them released and "signed off" before the clock ran out. On this occasion it worked well, but a couple of days later we were down to the wire before Bluey dismissed the five people on call. As I followed them up to my office, I wound my watch back by three minutes (no digital watches—old fashioned clockwork). By the time the extras handed me their chits for signature, they were rightly claiming payment for another half an hour.

"No," I said. "It's not yet five o'clock."

"Yes, it is," they countered as they offered up their watches for my inspection.

I showed them mine. "We go by this, and it's one minute to five," I told them firmly.

They had no choice but quietly to accept my decision. Golly, how proud I felt—I'd saved the company a total of about four pounds (by current standards maybe a hundred). As I drove home that evening preparing to tell Heather how clever I had been, a thought struck me—a ghastly thought. I was nothing more than a cheat and a liar who had done those people out of their fairly earned money. And there was no way Hammer would have approved of such a thing. The lesson I learned made me resolve never to cheat or lie again. It placed me on firm ground and shortly gave me the reputation of being a straight-up guy. The result was that, if any employee tried to con a production I was involved with, even the unions would invariably come down on my side. The gratitude I feel toward those five extras for behaving with such dignity when they knew I was in the wrong is as strong as it ever was.

Having graduated to junior management, I was now entitled to enjoy a privilege: Mrs T's wonderful lunches in the restaurant. Like every other studio, Bray had the basic canteen and the more private room. Both of these were a mini version, and the restaurant could accommodate no more than a dozen people. Mrs T's meals were exactly to the taste of an English schoolboy's palate and were served within the digestible space of a shooting crew's lunch break. I have always had a liking for chilled rosé, and the excellent stock of the wine at Bray was slowly consumed, largely by me. It had been ordered onto the premises by Anthony Hinds, who, on a rare visit to the studio, found none of his favorite was available.

The bit of doggerel dreamed up by the publicity department as a tagline for *The Mummy's Shroud*, "Beware the beat of the cloth-wrapped feet!" just about sums up the whole. Maggie Kimberley, recently divorced out of the South African diamond family, gave, with judicious editing, an acceptable performance as the girl in jeopardy and Michael Ripper excelled in his role of "Longbarrow," who meets with a spooky death. Eddie Powell portrayed the mummy convincingly (if a walking one can ever be convincing). Also in the cast was the distinguished André Morell, who, sad to say, was not very pleasant to me. Ideally during close-ups, an actor should have the person he is playing a scene with standing to one side of the camera to feed him or her lines and give them someone to react to. This is not always possible. In one instance, as I had often done before, I took up the off-screen position of the absent actor André was supposedly talking to. Just before the camera rolled, he called out to me aggressively, "If you stand there, I'll kill you!"

"But I was just giving you your eye-line," I responded as I moved away, consoling myself with the thought that aggressiveness is usually a sign of insecurity.

As enjoyable as this film was to make (apart from that moment), it was about to be eclipsed by one of my all-time favorites.

· 4 ·

Wow!

Three august gentlemen were sitting around Anthony Nelson Keys's outer office—ANK himself, Terence Fisher, and director Roy Baker—and I was there too. Over an evening drink, we were discussing "tricks of the trade" when it came to foreign locations. My elders put forward their theories for ensuring comfort and then it came to my turn. "I always wear disposable underpants," I told them as a matter of fact, and as matter-of-factly as seemed appropriate.

"What?" said Terry, chuckling in delighted disbelief.
"Yes," I continued, "it saves on laundry bills."
"But don't they fall apart?"
"No, the material's a bit like kitchen cloths."
"Good Lord!"
"And there's a bonus, you can blow your nose on them before disposal—saves on Kleenex."
"HE-eeh!" put in Roy Baker in a sound of amusement that I would get to know so well over the years.
"And you're the one who's against too much paperwork, young man," said Mr. Keys dryly.
"Might try them myself," Terry murmured.

Terry was at the studio polishing off the postproduction of the latest Frankenstein, and Roy Baker there to discuss the next production scheduled for Hammer. Again I had been kept on after most others had left, to help clear up at Bray once and for all. Doubtless the cost of running it for fifty-two weeks a year had become more expensive than renting space at another studio for the duration of shooting, and so, very sadly, the mummy picture was the last one we made there. But the future held promise over at Elstree.

Although I hadn't been offered the assignment, I had reason to hope that I might be asked to join the crew of *Quatermass and the Pit*, which Roy was to make. Much had been said about his irascibility (some claiming it was a condition brought about by his slight physical stature and his red hair), but to be realistic, he simply couldn't tolerate sloppiness. However, I decided, it would be as well to watch my p's and q's around him.

Many years later, I was to produce, with John Hawkesworth, the television series *The Flame Trees of Thika,* starring Hayley Mills, which Roy directed in Kenya. One sequence had to be filmed just as the sun was slipping beyond the horizon—something that happens very rapidly on the equator. "Right, we'll shoot now!" called Roy.

"Stand by," called the first assistant director.

"Hang on a minute," piped up the sound recordist (sound recordists always seem to fiddle with wires at the last moment).

"I haven't got a fucking minute," yelled Roy, turning puce with anger. "Roll the fucking camera!"

And he got the shot just as darkness fell.

Having been privileged to write a few words to accompany his recent autobiography, I take the liberty of repeating them here:

> A word to the wise, a cliché though it may be, we will ever learn from history. Roy Ward Baker's autobiography *The Director's Cut* entertains from start to finish. Of equal importance is the fact that it shows the evolution of the medium through the eyes of a prolific filmmaker during the second half of the last century. From this we can learn how it attained maturity. This book is necessary reading for all students of film be they in their twenties or eighties.

Although I had not met Roy Baker until that evening at Bray, I had heard of him through my father and the "Pinewood connection" and more particularly because of three of his admirable films: *Morning Departure,* with the all-engrossing tension created by men trapped at the bottom of the sea in a submarine; *The One That Got Away,* the wartime story of a German airman escaping from a British prisoner of war camp—dangerous stuff, because the audience sympathy is with the German; and *A Night to Remember,* the definitive film of the sinking of the *Titanic*, which even now leaves the more recent telling of the story pitifully in the shade.

For the time being, a few more words about Roy: He is a highly educated man and a supreme storyteller.

Nineteen sixty-six had been a busy year and my tutoring intense, so I was happy to take Heather to my parents' home in Italy for Christmas. It is a lovely place on the Costa dei Fiori, the house standing next door to the world-renowned Hanbury Gardens at La Mortola di Ventimiglia. It was a time to relax and play, while keeping my fingers crossed about future employment—and it was a very special time because Heather was expecting our first child.

My hopes for work came to fruition when, in late January, ANK telephoned and asked me to join the unit of *Quatermass* as the second assistant director. Wow! The highlight of my career had arrived. There was, however, a tricky situation to be overcome: my potential disruption of an existing team. Generally it is important to keep as many people working together over as long a period of time as possible, because so much more can be done by intuition rather than verbal communication and my position as second assistant to Bert Batt could have upset a status quo. Naturally, this concerned me.

Bert was the epitome of the first assistant (and more besides, including his work as the screenwriter of *Frankenstein Must Be Destroyed*—although a calamity nearly came about over that script). His regularly established second assistant was a man called Dusty Symonds. By breaking up their unity, I was in danger of alienating myself from the outset with Bert and risking Dusty's accusation that he was being usurped, which in a way he was by Mr. Keys's decision to employ me in his place. A visit to the set of the production they were currently working on at Pinewood immediately allayed my doubts. Dusty could not have been more generous in encouraging me to go ahead and assured me that he was off to do something else anyway. This proved to be so, and there might have been a side of him that was happy to escape the constant, though perfectly justifiable, demands made by his immediate superior.

In a way, Bert suffered from tunnel vision. All that mattered in the world to him—all—was the picture he was responsible for. A heavy smoker, with a dry sense of humor and a dry attitude to alcohol (except on one notable occasion when in crisis, he resorted to a small glass of lager), he was very much the type to lead a unit. With three leaders on the crew—Roy Baker, camera operator Moray Grant, and Bert—we were potentially on the edge of an avalanche.

As usual, my letter of engagement arrived (the salary more than I had expected) along with the script by "Tom" Kneale, based on his own television series of a decade earlier. What a good script it was, apart from one element observed only in retrospect.

Although not yet on the payroll, I was unable to resist settling down to plot out my end of the production.

We should have been based at the Associated British Pictures Corporation Studios in Borehamwood, considering Hammer's distribution relationship with the studio's parent company, but the place was full with their own productions. So we got bumped up the road to M-G-M. Borehamwood (sometimes referred to as "Bore'em stiff") is now quite a large town, a short way out of the pretty Hertfordshire village of Elstree, and emerged purely as a result of film industry activities. Although by the 1960s it was declining as the Hollywood of England, in its past it had seen British International Pictures on one lot and British and Dominion (which was destroyed by fire in 1936) on another, and then there were the Gate Studios and National Studios. And for a short while, it included the New Elstree Studios, run by the Danziger Brothers, where they made third- or fourth-rate B pictures.

Metro-Goldwyn-Mayer, like most other American majors, had set up shop in England as a means of getting around British Film Quota laws—but that's another story. As it happened, their studio was one of the best places in the country to make movies. No, it didn't have the charm of Shepperton or the character of Pinewood, but it was designed intelligently for use by filmmakers and was a highly efficient and happy place in which to work. Although much older, ABPC (Borehamwood) was not remotely as well thought out and had a reputation of unease and union problems. So we were really lucky.

The only other producer working "just up the road" alongside us was Stanley Kubrick, who was extensively filming the special effects sequences for *2001: A Space Odyssey*—fascinating to watch if one could go AWOL for a short period or two and get onto his stage.

Virtually all of our production was shot within Metro's boundaries—the interiors on the excellent sound stages and the exteriors a few hundred yards away on the lot. Already standing there was a large street set, which had been used in countless movies before. I don't know which was the first of them, but I'm willing to bet it supposedly took place in France. Look at Hobb's End in *Quatermass* and you cannot fail to notice the mansard roofs of Paris.

Bernie Robinson surpassed himself with our underground set, a train station under construction as far as the plot was concerned, which was just as well since it meant there was no need to have trains running through! It could not have been more real, with mountains of soggy clay from the tunnel digging at either end; the circular sides and roof reflecting the "workers" arc lights and the very real drip-drip-dripping of seeping water.

A lengthy retelling of the story is unwarranted here as anyone who knows anything about Hammer Films will be familiar with it. However, simply for the few who are not:

> Whilst excavating the tunnel for a new subway line beneath London, workmen discover a strange missile. A bomb disposal officer is brought in, along with Professor Quatermass. Inside are satanic looking creatures—aliens from another planet? And do they hold the key to the dawn of man? Whatever, there is an unwanted force present, and panic in the city breaks out as poltergeists begin a reign of destruction. Quatermass must find a scientific way of discharging the evil.

The eponymous hero was played by the forty-year-old Andrew Keir, one of our regulars. This large, bearded Scotsman, who always called people of my age "son," was not a star in the real sense, but his numerous performances in many other films are well remembered. The part of Quatermass fitted him like a neat glove, and he managed to bring out a range of emotions most successfully.

James Donald, another Scotsman, was a very watchable actor, although tending to play his character, the anthropologist, Dr. Roney, on one level. In fact this was his style and exactly how he performed the end scene in *The Bridge on the River Kwai*—"Madness, madness," says Major Clipton in neutral voice after the bridge has been destroyed. He will also be remembered in a similar way in *The Great Escape*.

Barbara Shelley was cast as his assistant. This was the least interesting role, and she must have struggled with it; consequently she was not up to her usual earthiness. It is sad so little has been seen of her since *Quatermass*.

Julian Glover, a prominent Shakespearean actor who was later to appear in *Indiana Jones and the Last Crusade* and *Star Wars—The Empire Strikes Back,* as well as masses of other films, was the bomb disposal officer, Colonel Breen. At the time we thought he might have been a bit young for a colonel, but so convincing was he that, if it were true, it was instantly forgotten. A short way into the production, he was to do something most kind and thoughtful, however simple, and I still remember it today, frequently mentioning it when introducing him to a friend.

One of the principal responsibilities of a second assistant is to make sure that the actors are "called" for the following day's work (as against the third's job of getting them from the dressing rooms to the stage) and that they are fully aware of what time to be at the studio. Men were usually allowed half an hour in makeup and hairdressing (except in the case of prosthetics), and women an hour. This normally sufficed (except in the case of one actress I was to encounter, who took six hours to be readied). So, on average, the makeup department and the second assistant would be at the studio by around 7:00 A.M. Now the absolute rule about "calling" was that the actor had to be informed *personally,* and a plague on a second if this was not adhered to. That was fine if the actor was already present in the studio, but otherwise it was the telephone. One small part player hadn't answered his phone by the time I was off home to my very pregnant wife (in fact Heather was eight days overdue). I tried again from home—no reply. Again at 10:00 P.M.—no. At 11:00 P.M.—nothing. We had to go to bed, the drive to the studio would take an hour in the morning, and before leaving I had the fire to lay and light (no central heating then). Well, thank God for manual telephone exchanges. From the cottage where we lived, there was no dial; we simply had to lift the receiver and wait for the operator. (This had many advantages over the modern system—on one occasion someone was trying to contact me when the Fulmer Village operator advised him to try again in five minutes because he'd just seen me go past the exchange window on my way home.) Fortunately Frank Williams was on duty that night.

"Frank, help. Can you keep trying this actor's number and when he answers ring me, no matter the time?"

"Pleased to, Chris," he responded. Nice chap Frank; I'd known him since childhood, his elderly mother had been my mother's housekeeper.

Off to bed. . . . Just dozing off. . . . Ringgggg. . . . Frank had got the actor. "Oh, yes, I already know," he informed me, "I called the office earlier."

No one in the office had bothered to tell me.
Just dozing off again....
A groan, followed by a sort of yelp. "What is it?"
"A pain in my back," said Heather.
"I'll rub it."
This seemed to help for a while. Then another yelp.... By now we knew what was happening. We got to the convent nursing home, adjacent to good old Beaconsfield Studios, where Heather was to give birth, and within fifteen minutes she had undergone confirmatory tests. For an expectant father to be present throughout the procedure in the 1960s was uncommon, and indeed frowned upon by the medical staff and the nuns. They did not want some useless person hanging around, who was likely to faint at the sight of blood—imagine someone working for Hammer fainting at that! Anyway, by five in the morning, I left.

Early at the studio. Watched the March sky lighten above the parking lot and thought, rather romantically, "This is the break of the day when my child enters this world."

By seven o'clock final preparations were underway for shooting. And would you believe it, the actor who'd kept me up late for half the previous night was the first to appear!

A big scene was about to start on the lot—people running, ducking, falling as the evil poltergeists unleash their wrath (for what reason I was never quite sure). Buildings collapsing, rubble strewn willy-nilly, men and women dashed to the ground with liberal splashings of Kensington Gore.

Phone call to the nursing home—Heather was "one finger," whatever prenatal meaning that had.

Seventy-five extras to be repositioned.

"Two fingers...."

The day was moving on, and I was exhausted. "Here you are," said the unit nurse as she handed me a glass of water and two pills. "Purple hearts."

"They're 'uppers,' aren't they?"

"You need an upper, it's okay."

Popped them.

Telephone, "Three fingers," said Sister Basil.

"How much longer?"

"We really can't say."

Why couldn't they say? Surely they were experienced in estimating labor time—godammit, after all, we had to estimate how long it would take to film a section of London collapsing—surely more unusual than childbirth.... I slapped my impatient wrists.

Message from Bert Batt via the third assistant director, "Get the guys from the last shot cleaned up.... I need twenty-five freshened extras in fifteen minutes."

Wardrobe department, makeup department....

"Tell Bernie we need another truck of rubble for the next shot—ten minutes...." I allocated the assignment to a gofer. My duty was to book one hundred and fifty extras for the next day's scenes of mayhem.

Crazy.... The British government had introduced one of its more ridiculous taxation schemes. Selective Employment Tax (SET) ruled that if anyone were to be employed for more than eight hours a week, a surcharge was implemented. To avoid this liability, we had to have an entirely new set of people for the crowd scenes each day. Phone, phone, phone....

And the phone again.... "Four fingers. The baby should be with us in just a short while," said the Irish voice.

"What's a short while?"

My pulse was racing at 5:20 P.M. when Bert called the "wrap."

A mass of people changed out of filthy costumes and came along to my office to be "signed off" for payment. About three had passed through when the next one claimed "special action" payment. I looked at the man standing to my left—a dark-haired and fairly stout character who was known to be an active shop steward.

"Name?" Norman North asked the claimant.

"[So-and-so]."

"You're not on the list."

I looked quizzically at the taller man to my right—also a shop steward. "Fred?"

Shaking his head, he said, "Not on my list either."

I signed the voucher without additional payment. No arguments—there couldn't be. What I'd set up was a system, which was carefully explained to everyone involved beforehand. Should any extra believe he had done more work than simply turn up for the day, he had to advise one of the stewards at the time of the scene in question. If the latter felt it to be fair, he would make a note of it along with the recommended amount of reward. The result was no lengthy arguments at the end of the day.

Twenty more people came through the system—a good seventy-five behind them. My phone rang.

As I replaced the receiver, I said out loud, "I've just become the father of a little boy."

There was an instant round of applause.

I presented myself at seven-thirty in the evening at the nursing home, to be greeted by the indefatigable Sister Basil, and shortly I held the minute Gareth Elwin Neame in my arms. It was the most complete moment in my life.

(Sister Basil, the Irish nun with whom I had been in communication all day, was a splendid soul with a merry sense of humor. Apparently, on September 30 every year, she was known to stand by the entry of the delivery room. Hands tucked into the wide sleeves of her black habit, she would smile at each young woman wheeled past her on a trolley and remark, "You must have had a very happy New Year's Eve, my dear.")

Zonked, I was in bed by nine o'clock and hoping Heather, who must have been even more exhausted, was by now getting some sleep. A few hours later I was back at Metro for another hard stint as more "Londoners" had their city destroyed around them.

On my way up to the exterior set, I met Julian Glover, and somewhat unceremoniously he handed me a brown paper package. "This is for your son, with love." It was a tiny little all-in-one outfit—so thoughtful of him, and it has endeared him to me for life.

Life comes and goes. A few evenings later, as the extras were being paid off, one of them collapsed and died. It came as a shock and saddened me greatly—he had been part of my team and, in a way, I felt responsible. Perhaps I had asked him to exert more energy than he was capable of sustaining.

The rubble that was being hurled into the blast of aircraft engines by propmen, assistant directors, and stagehands, was, of course, harmless—just great chunks of polystyrene, painted grey or brick-colored, with the crashing sounds to be added later. Having said that, I need to mention that there were a few real bits of concrete and bricks around in some areas that weren't supposed to be blown away. It was bound to happen, I suppose. . . . A jolly side-sport for those waiting for a shot to be set up was to kick the polystyrene around like a football. One young man took a running kick at a real bit of concrete. Broke his foot, naturally!

Bert Batt had to leave the production three days before the end to start preparing our next film, which was for Jimmy Sangster—another name synonymous with Hammer. So I was upgraded to first assistant. It was a great kindness on the part of Roy Baker to allow me to take charge of just about everything except the positioning of the camera. "Action!" I called loudly, for the first time in my life. And the extras started fleeing from the evil force. . . .

"Go, Pete!" was the cue for part of a building to start tumbling. Two seconds later, "Go, Johnny!" and a mass of debris came in from the right. "Norman, go!" and Norman North led a swathe of extras past the camera. "Syd, go!" So on and so forth.

I learned a considerable amount from this, particularly in timing the moments of action correctly. Thank you, Roy, for giving me the opportunity.

Undeniably the movie has "legs," and it really is extraordinary to read reviews for *Quatermass* written very recently, some thirty-five years after the picture was made. A word common to most is "excellent." While working on this book, I have played video copies of many of the films and, in the case of this one, would like to add one more review, if it can be called such, of my own.

Originally it seemed that Roy Baker had it going along at too rapid a pace, but now it seems slow. TV commercials and pop promos have taught audiences many signals that replace the lengthy exposition needed then. Nevertheless, despite the leisurely pace, I did become a bit lost about who was doing what to whom in the story and why.

Andrew Keir is still superb, and I was surprised at how effective James Donald remains. Barbara Shelley worked too hard—her difficulty was, in my opinion, created by the only character flaw in the script. Who is it she is playing? Where does she come from? Does she have a life outside her work with Dr. Roney? Married, divorced, or single? Has she a lover? These are the things a performer needs to know to create a character, even if the audience witnesses none of it. The big surprise was

Duncan Lamont, as a workman who is the first to be afflicted by the aliens. His portrayal of the jabbering wreck of a man he becomes as a result is entirely believable. (One of those actors to be seen in lots of Hammer films, Duncan was another to die far too young.) And Tristram Carey's musical score pitches in at a very high standard.

The aliens, themselves, don't stand the test of time—they look like bundles of green foam rubber, vaguely shaped like locusts and oozing green paint. However, the surreal image of one of them in the night sky over London toward the end is still tremendous because of its lack of definition and its simplicity (a Les Bowie masterpiece). Julian Glover's crumbling demise also hits the mark. However, generally speaking, far too much makeup was used in the 1960s—men covered in the stuff—and this dates the film. Something that doesn't date the film is the dress of the women extras, who always wore their own clothes. On the express orders of ANK, none were to be seen in the then newly-in-vogue miniskirts. Great pity, but the idea was to avoid setting the story in any given time. I think this was wrong—the time was clearly mid-sixties, and it might have done well to expose a bit of leg here and there.

From the standpoint of a second assistant, *Quatermass* had been a very busy production, but on looking at it now, there seems to be only about a quarter of the number of people that we dressed into the scenes of pandemonium. Why should this be? I can only think it is similar to an adult who revisits a place from childhood and always finds it smaller than memory would allow.

One footnote about the currently available video of *Quatermass*: Until Hollywood decided to acknowledge everyone who stepped within ten miles of the cameras, screen credits were kept to a minimum and were invariably presented at the beginning of a film. Presumably, so as to keep pace with trends, the *Quatermass* titles now appear at the end over a two-shot of the drained but successful Andrew Keir and Barbara Shelley. Ludicrous. Running the shot backwards and forwards in order to lengthen it as a background leaves these two with egg on their faces as they continuously repeat their facial movements.

However, at the time we finished at M-G-M, in 1967 I was still saying "Wow!"

· 5 ·

BD

"*F*ire him" were the only words she said in response to "What a lovely day, Miss Davis." Not having been present, I cannot vouch for the accuracy of the quote, but it was what Bette Davis was supposed to have said on arrival at Southampton. She had come to star in *The Nanny* for Hammer. The poor man, who was subsequently removed from the picture (but not his regular employment at the studio), was one of the publicity men at ABPC. The star hated small talk and, boy, had she demonstrated it. I know nothing about this film other than the fact that the wife of the producer, Jimmy Sangster, threatened divorce if he were ever to work with Miss Davis again. Both happened.

The day after I finished up the road at Metro, I joined Bert as his second assistant on the last days of preparation for *The Anniversary*. Another great, though daunting, opportunity was approaching—working with one of Hollywood's biggest stars.

"This one's going to be a doddle," Bert remarked to me. It definitely seemed likely. Based on a stage play by Bill MacIlwraith, the principal cast, headed by BD, numbered six, with five additional parts and one restaurant scene with extras. Shooting would be done on a composite set of a large house on the stage, plus two nights of exteriors around a bonfire up on the lot and half a day on location at the house the company had rented for Miss Davis from Stanley Kubrick. Still, I remember at the time wishing Bert had not tempted fate. And, as it turned out, he had.

Two days later we were doing makeup tests on our leading lady. Portraying a wealthy woman who continued to manipulate her grown-up children, she had sophisticated costumes—and, of all things, an eye patch. During the story we learn that her eye had been shot out inadvertently by one of her sons. This patch could have been a problem, indeed even dangerous, because one-eyed vision is two-dimensional, hampering judgment of distances. Also, in the case of actors, it would make it difficult for them to "feel" their camera position mark precisely and this had to be precise, for reasons of lighting and focus. The difficulty was dealt with by cutting away the center of her patch and placing thin black material over the surface—and, on the day of the widowed Mrs Taggart's anniversary, scarlet red. So in actual fact Bette Davis could see perfectly well throughout the production.

The director of photography for *The Anniversary* was Harry Waxman. Excellent, though not right in the top line of cameramen, he was recognized throughout the industry as being the most technically learned. His only fault was that he could get himself worked up too easily; nevertheless, when it came to lighting Miss Davis, we were on very safe ground. Alvin Rakoff, a young Canadian, was our director; his background had been in television.

An extraordinary American woman, with a big floppy bag, floppy shoes, and a harsh tongue, had come over with her to look after Miss Davis's interests throughout. On the first morning Viola Rubber preceded her onto the stage to check things out. She looked around with critical eyes and exclaimed something like, "My! Oh, my!" and turned to me.

"Young man, this will never do."

"What, Miss Rubber?" I asked in all innocence.

"All these hundreds of wires around the floor. You'll have to get them shifted so there's no risk of Miss Davis tripping."

"We can't. They're the cables feeding electricity to the lamps."

Obviously she had never set foot in a studio before.

"They're still highly dangerous."

"I think Miss Davis will manage; she will have been stepping over them all her life."

"Humphh!" retorted the displeased Miss Rubber as she made her way off to collect her charge.

"Good morning, everyone," said BD brightly and sweetly when she arrived on the set.

So far so good, I thought, as she took up her position in front of the camera. "Hello, Harry." Harry had photographed her in *The Nanny* and she obviously liked him. It all flowed so simply—she angled herself immediately into her key-light, raised her chin, then lowered it, brought it back to the level, paused and raised it slightly. This was what Harry needed to see—how she looked at her best and how she would actually hold her head as the character she was to portray. Without a word spoken between them, Harry raised the key-light about one and a half inches.

We carried on like this all day, with adjustments being made by makeup artist George Partleton, an avuncular soul with a garden-gnome face and a neat little bristly moustache. Scottie, the hairdresser, and wardrobe mistress Mary Gibson did their bit, too. All went well for most of us; it was just Viola Rubber who seemed to get into some trouble from her boss for fussing too much.

That evening I went to the star's dressing room in accordance with my responsibilities. "Miss Davis, your makeup call for Monday morning is seven-thirty, ready on set for eight-forty-five."

She turned to me and again smiled sweetly. "Okay, kid, but you don't need to tell me. Just put down the time you want me ready on the call sheet—my driver will collect a copy from the unit office."

She smiled benignly once again as she turned back to her dressing room mirror and applied a dollop of Pond's cream to remove her makeup. The last thing I heard as I closed the door behind me was, "Viola, pour me another drink, if you please."

The old rigid rule, drummed into me by ANK, came to the forefront of my mind. Whether or not an actor refused their "call time" or even if they spat in your face, the second assistant was obliged to deliver the information personally. Not to worry now, a summer weekend with my wife and baby son lay ahead.

Monday. Miss Davis was on set twenty minutes before we required her and, without saying a word, sat on a production chair at a respectful distance from the camera. I wish I could say this ideal attendance applied to all the other members of the cast. Jack Hedley, James Cossins, and Sheila Hancock were most professional, but the younger ones inclined to be rather bothersome—obviously they felt they had "arrived" as actors and would ensure their status was upheld—if only by themselves.

Early in the afternoon, Miss Rubber came to me and said Miss Davis required a dressing room on the stage. I was a bit lost at first, but the art department came to my rescue by stepping in and erecting four flats, one with a door and a roof piece. And by five o'clock it was furnished with a couch, easy chair, dressing table, full-length mirror, and carpet. "That way,

Miss Davis will be close at hand when you need her." I was amazed by the simplicity of the request (and the common sense behind it) as there were many stories about how major stars wanted a suite of dressing rooms, freshly painted and newly carpeted—not just some box with a bit of set dressing in a corner of the stage.

Five-thirty at the door of Miss Davis's principal dressing room: "Come in," quavered the famous voice from beyond.

There she was, before the mirror, lashings of Pond's cream and a big whisky.

"Listen, kid, I told you, you don't need to give me a call."

So I blurted out the "on set" time and, aware of Viola Rubber's scowl, left rapidly.

It was the call on the Tuesday night for the Wednesday that now promised to be very, very tricky. With seven and a half weeks to go, I opted for a bold knock at the door rather than sound too timid—so many people seemed to quake before BD that productions must have been a nightmare for them, but it wasn't the game for me—after all, hadn't I shown Gregory Peck how to play cricket?

"Come," she said imperiously and with a degree of suspicion.

This time she was alone in the room, but otherwise everything else was the same—including the Pond's cream and large whisky.

Irked by my persistence, she said. "Damn it, kid, how many times have I got to tell you not to come here?"

Okay. I realized this couldn't go on. Something had to give. Barriers had to be brought down. "So," I said, taking the bull by the horns, "getting pissed on your own tonight, are you, love."

She was as taken aback by my words as I was. Then she laughed in her smoker's husky way. "That's right kid. Sit down." She pointed to a nearby chair as she reached for a glass and poured me a slug. From then on we became chums. It was not a busy picture for me, and actors are always waiting for the next shot to be prepared, so in total we spent many hours together. It might have been telling jokes, talking about my new son, about her life in America and her family, or my childhood experiences in Hollywood, where I was partly brought up. And I never did give her another "call." She was always there beforehand. Sometimes I'd take a short lunch and be back on the stage in good time to hurry people along when they arrived. She was the first, and often before me. On my way home in the evening, I might drop by her house for a drink, and on one occasion when her companion was not present, she referred to her as "Rubble," insinuating, if I am correct, that poor old Viola was basically of Flintstone mentality and not much in favor.

That is one strand about the making of *The Anniversary*; another is a less happy event.

Alvin Rakoff was of the Sydney Newman School of (largely Canadian) television directors of the fifties and early sixties—and bloody good they were, too. However, their method of handling a project was vastly different from the standard way of approaching cinema. The first few days went well enough—or so it seemed, but Bette was uncomfortable with Alvin. What happened came without warning. He was taken off the picture at the end of the first week. All the crew felt deep sympathy for him. Bert, in a rare expression of emotion, hugged him, and we said our farewells. The gap had to be filled, and Jimmy Sangster, along with Anthony Hinds and everyone else who mattered at Hammer, made a wise and quick choice: Roy Baker. Although he had never worked with BD before, he knew her quite well in a social setting—their acquaintance made while he was working in LA with Marilyn Monroe on *Don't Bother to Knock*.

Obviously this meant that he would be splitting his time between editing *Quatermass* and taking over a new production. He handled the situation with aplomb and got his own way into the bargain. In fairness, there really wasn't much to criticize about Alvin's footage, but a replacement director would prefer to start from scratch. Roy took one look at the principal set and declared that the staircase, which ran from the right of the hallway of Mrs. Taggart's house up to the left, was the wrong way round. He required it to go from (camera) bottom left up to the right. His preference defied argument; if it was what he wanted in order to take over the film, then that was what he would have. All very clever—he bought himself time and ensured that what had already been shot was confined to the cutting room bin, permanently. One can have nothing but admiration for his deft political maneuver. While the set was reconstructed over the following week, my lawn and various other things at home received extra attention.

I didn't discuss the situation with BD when we returned to work—not my place—but she had clearly been unhappy about the development of the project and needed the change. It must have been ghastly for

Alvin, but he has had a distinguished career ever since and there was no long-lasting damage done. Or was there? The pain of being "released" from a picture runs deep, whatever the circumstances, even though the bottom line is usually attributable to creative differences rather than incompetence.

Any air of gloom hanging over the set was rapidly dispersed by a line from Sheila Hancock, who played Jack Hedley's wife. Coming down the by now famous staircase, she passes one of her brothers-in-law—James Cossins. His character has a perverted streak, and a particular fetish was snatching ladies' undergarments from washing lines. The Taggart family are property developers and builders of questionable quality and, as the two pass each other, he informs her he is going off to lay some floorboards. Sheila ad-libbed, "Make the most of it, that's all you'll ever lay." The instant laughter helped pick the crew up.

But tensions soon ran high again as news broke of what was to become known as the Six Day War. Fifty-six-year-old Harry Waxman's Jewish blood boiled—he was off to fight for Israel. Fortunately he was persuaded to "give it a couple of days" to cool off. But so volatile were his inner feelings that anything could trigger a local war. And it did.

"Just move forward to your closer position," said the camera focus assistant as he stretched a measuring tape level with one of the actor's eyes immediately prior to a take.

Roy Baker went ballistic.

He is adamant that there is only one person on a film set who gives instructions to the performers—the director. Categorically no one else. Only through him should anything be communicated. Whether his outburst was justified is another matter, but the result was the instant departure from the stage of a deeply hurt assistant, who would claim he had just been doing his job. And his already impassioned senior left in support.

Murmurings went on, feet shuffled and Bette quietly retired to her dressing room on the stage. A good half hour passed before Jimmy Sangster managed to calm the situation down. Roy was obliged to apologize publicly in order to avoid everything grinding to a complete halt. He did so in good grace, but, knowing him well enough by now, I picked up a minute tightening of his jaw muscles. Looking back on it, I'd have to say Roy overreacted, but in the moments prior to "Action!" a director has to be the sole communicator between the actor and the outside world. Ultimately the director is the actor's audience and should command his or her entire attention, and vice versa. Difficult one, though.

Another strained day, but we finished it on schedule.

Roy's bark is worse than his bite, but there has always been an exciting danger about him. Let me be very clear about this statement. My admiration for him as a director remains undiminished and, over the years, he has always proved to be a congenial dining partner and friend, but at work he expected to be obeyed and, one day in the summer of 1967, I had reason to query his instruction. The daily "call sheet" always bears the same heading—title of film—date—and the name of the director.

"From now on, put me down as Roy Ward Baker," he said.

"What?" Here was a well-established "name" changing his name.

"Yes," he affirmed.

"Why? I mean why should you want to do that?"

He looked as if he were going to get angry.

"My mother's maiden name," he eventually said, "and I'm fed up to the back teeth with being confused with Roy Baker, the sound editor."

"It's a bit drastic, isn't it?"

Anyway, director Don Sharp had stuck with his name even though there was a sound editor called Don Sharp.

"That's what I've decided," said Roy Baker.

I duly made the amendment and even gave him a draft copy, risking the words, "Are you really sure?"

"Why should I not be?"

Thirty years later he told me, "One of the worst decisions I ever made." All the excellent movies he had directed before have gone down in history as the work of someone else!

With the Arab-Israeli war behind us, we at last started the glide toward the end of the schedule and Bert Batt's "doddle" started to emerge at long last. We even celebrated July 4th on set with Bette dressed up as a daughter of Uncle Sam. Then a couple of night exteriors round a bonfire on the lot and we'd be about done.

There are plusses and minuses about shooting at night in the English summer, depending on your point of view. It's a short night, 9:00 P.M.

to, say, 4:30 A.M., meaning fewer hours of work for the crew, but also fewer hours for filming. Even in the country's warmest season, it can be chilly, and so a trailer was provided for the cast to relax in—but not BD. She opted to stay her normal twenty feet back from the camera, benefiting from the glow of the bonfire.

On the second night, she was asked to be up on the lot at 8:45 P.M., and, as usual, she was ready and waiting at the studio entrance—but her car and driver weren't. They were nowhere to be seen and, in order to protect her costume, she needed transportation. Only one thing for it.

"I'll drive you up there."

"Right," she replied.

A minute later I had my maroon mini outside the door, and gamely she started clambering in.

Jimmy Sangster appeared; "What's happening?"

I explained.

"I'll drive Miss Davis up there."

So she got out of my car and into Jimmy's much more fitting Bentley—winking at me as she did so.

What Jimmy did was absolutely correct, and if my recounting of the above suggests otherwise, it is quite wrong. Just an amusing experience, with an important star playing with the kid on the block—of course she should have been afforded better quality transport.

I seem to be referring frequently to the kindness and supportiveness of those I encountered at Hammer, but it wasn't always that way; every community has its share of shits. But Jimmy Sangster was positively not one of them. He was quintessentially Hammer (and I only speak of him in the past tense because here he belongs to Hammer's heyday). If he were to be eclipsed by anyone, it would have been Colonel Carreras. However, the latter was a supreme salesman, whereas Jimmy was a filmmaker. Although rising to the heights of writer, producer, and eventually director, Jimmy was never elevated to executive status, and I doubt he would have wanted it. This is probably no bad thing, as he was not made of the right material, being more the perennial schoolboy. It started with his boyish grin, an endearing quality I've only seen as vividly in one other grown man—Graham Greene—with the twinkling eyes of a mischievous ten-year-old in short trousers. Jimmy dresses as well now as he did then in a casual, yet quality way.

Somehow jeans, mid-length hair, and, at one time, a Zapata moustache suited the persona.

Jimmy has written several books about his experiences in the film industry and in particular Hammer, so it would be wrong for me to retell any of his story here. Suffice it to say, he started at the bottom and rose to become an assistant director and then production manager. He seems to have been around (and cheap) when a script needed writing, and so he did an adaptation of a Victor Canning novel, and then his original *X The Unknown*. This was of the *Quatermass* genre and, in its day, a very scary movie. Special effects were at the very minimum on the cost scale and no doubt that's why it all worked so well. The audience was left to imagine what Hammer couldn't afford to show on screen—and how much more exciting that often is, on screen, with horror as with sex. All that was needed was a good script and the "punters" could be left to do the rest. It's a moot point; should you give people what they want in full computerized glory, or hold back? Both can be effective, but they have to be in the right hands.

Jimmy was an adept creator. His many other credits include *Dracula* (the very best of Hammer), *The Curse of Frankenstein,* and *Fear in the Night*. He has remained self-deprecating about this last one (mind you, that's in his nature about most things he has done), but the actual making of it was another of those highly exhilarating moments in my life—some years on from *The Anniversary*.

It was he who started me on the road to production management. After a couple of weeks of shooting with BD, and during less fraught times, I went to his ever-open office.

"Jimmy," I said—using his name rather than calling him "sir," which wouldn't have suited him anyway (and I was growing up by then), "for the next four weeks, at least, we've got the same actors on the same set at the same time, so I don't have a thing to do. What else can we get on with?"

"You can do me a schedule for my next picture."

"I don't know how."

He explained the method in his laconic way and let me try it out. It was a script he'd adapted from his own novel, *Private Eye*. A while later *The Spy Killer*, as it became known, went into production at Pinewood, starring Michael Horton with Roy Ward Baker as director. Unfortunately I was unable to be part of it, because, at the time, I was involved with a Hollywood TV series that Hammer was commissioned to make for Twentieth Century Fox.

A schedule is the key to mounting any production. From it can be determined the amount of time actors will be required, how many sets have to be built, and how much location work there is. From the schedule, the budget can be estimated. It sounds straightforward enough, although in reality it's quite complex. This extracurricular activity kept me amused for two weeks, and more learning for me came in the process.

Then came the sad day when we said our adieus to Bette. I was never to see her again. There was one consolation though. My father, Ronnie, was at a mid-1970s industry event in Beverly Hills and she was there. He introduced himself to her and mentioned me. "Oh, Chris," she said. "Please do send him my very warmest wishes." And she laughed in her inimitable way. "We had a lot of fun together."

· 6 ·

No Cowboys!

A crashed nineteen-twenties Lancia roadster, a seriously damaged Arriflex movie camera, and ditto a very special Mitchell camera were part of my induction into directing. Already aware of the first two calamities, I happened to mention the third to Terry Fisher as we stood together in the men's room at Elstree Studios. Terry thought for a moment and then started shaking with that laugh of his.

"I was thinking of not coming back to the studio this evening," I told him, rather morosely.

"I'm glad you did," he said as he wiped away his tears, "but don't worry. It's all insured."

Do you see what I mean? This wonderful man couldn't help lightening every situation.

Terry went his mirthful way down a corridor while I went in the opposite direction to explain to ANK the latest disaster to have befallen me on *The Devil Rides Out*.

It all began innocently enough when, on completion of *The Anniversary*, Bert and I rejoined Mr. Keys—same studio, change of offices, and fresh stages going at a discount price because no one wanted to film on them. ABPC had built a new block especially designed for burgeoning television production. Unfortunately, it was a bit of a white elephant. Television companies were in-house setups and were still bound up in restrictive union practices (only to be overcome by Margaret Thatcher's government in the 1980s), and this meant that no company would dare venture outside its own premises into an ostensibly freelance studio, even in the event of overcrowding. Another reason these stages were unloved was that the architects and the owners of ABPC must have declined the design input of those who would work out of them. Assuredly it defied logic—how could anyone have thought it smart to put a parking garage under the sound stages, so that engines starting up could and quite often did resound in the middle of a shot? Added to this, ingress and egress of scenery was hampered by the limiting size of the doors. And the management was highly protective of its beautiful new floors, resisting, whenever possible, a few good nails to secure scenery flats.

Although it was sad to see its fairly recent near-demise, this studio had started life on the wrong foot. Built on the site of the old British International Pictures lot, the then new "film factory" suffered from earlier design faults. Stage entry and soundproofing were problematic, and a carpentry workshop was in entirely the wrong place. It had a run of rather proud, white-painted, art deco executive buildings more concerned with their own image than functioning properly. Then, too, despite its outward appearance, ABPC was unwelcoming, with admission strictly denied to those without an official invitation. Those staff permanently employed there were obliged to "clock in" if they were merely artisans or of even lower rank. As a freelance employee of Hammer, I wasn't required to do it, nor were my colleagues; we were considered to be officer material! Little wonder that here the regimentation worked to the detriment of both management and workers as they pulled in different directions.

Nevertheless, I still enjoyed my time there.

It is not unreasonable to suggest that novelist Dennis Wheatley and Hammer Films were natural partners. Wheatley's well-constructed stories provided ideal material for audiences to be swept up into a shadowy world, and one cannot help wondering why no more than a handful of movies have been made from his work.

A character common to many of his books is the Duc de Richleau—most easily described as being similar to Dracula's dogged opponent, Van Helsing, but instead of doing battle with a vampire, de Richleau battled the head man—the Devil himself. Christopher Lee starred in this good-guy role, defying the expected norm, and once again invested it with his special quality—entirely convincing. When evil is afoot one feels safe in his presence on screen. Also Christopher is an inherently intelligent man and has a tremendous natural elegance, both physically and in manner, and this came across in his performance.

The only problem I had with him on this production and vice versa was to do with the telephone on the stage. As a star, he received quite a lot of calls during the day, and as a second assistant, so did I. Elstree had a public address system, and when one or the other of us was wanted our name would come through the speakers—with a degree of distorted sound, Chris Lee and Chris Neame sound remarkably similar. We were forever taking each other's calls. Both of us are now known by most people as Christopher—something to do with growing older, I dare say, and in my case prompted by secretaries on the other end of a line saying to their bosses, "It's Chris-tine on the phone." Really! Did I ever sound like a Christine?

Also in the cast was Charles Gray, who brought an acid strength to the Satanist leader, Mocata. Then there was dear old Gwen Ffrangcon Davies as one of many witches and, as a special treat, the lovely Niké Arrighi, the damsel in distress, overpowered by the evil Mocata. She was only twenty and very pretty, her slender body and small breasts and short hair standing her in good stead to appear in a 1920s subject.

The only disappointment was the hunky Leon Greene in the role of de Richleau's friend, Rex. It was near the beginning of his film career and, having been an opera singer, he was still finding the transition to the more inner performances required in cinema a little tricky. In the final event, there was only one thing for it; he had to be re-voiced. Patrick Allen expertly handled this, but there is always a danger with any sort of re-voicing. Even when done by an actor over his own performance (usually for technical reasons) there's a certain disembodiedness about it. Someone standing in front of a microphone, even breathlessly running in place, can hardly match the visual action. The energy or adrenaline of a filmed performance in a particular environment is just about impossible to recapture. I find it hard to credit it, but there is a "school" today that actually seems to prefer the dubbed result (for example, one director that I encountered not so long ago—but he is a poor example of a storyteller!).

On *The Devil Rides Out*, ANK and Terry Fisher had no choice but to re-voice Leon. I felt sorry for him. As with Alvin Rakoff, it is a smack in the mouth when a person has given of his best and been rejected. But, also like Alvin, Leon went on to other things.

But slow up. I'm getting ahead of myself. Back to the shooting.

"Me?" I couldn't have sounded more incredulous.

"Yes," said Mr. Keys.

"Well, er. . . ."

"Well, er, what?"

"I don't know whether I'd be any good," I said weakly.

"You can't come to much harm, young *feller-me-lad*." (Unfortunately, he wasn't right about that!)

"Hope not. . . ."

He had called me into his office to propose that I direct the second unit. Direct—ee*ek*!

"You've a basic understanding of camera setups and you're passable at getting things organized," he said. Then he added, "Although you could more usefully keep a list of information and deliver two or three instructions at one time rather than individually. It'd save your feet and be more efficient."

The sequence I would be responsible for would see Tanith (Niké Arrighi) attempting to escape her rescuers to return to the hypnotic clutches of Mocata. She grabs a car and rushes off with Rex in hot pursuit in a second car. It ends with a crash. Car chases are very complex to film, with short cuts being essential to build up and sustain the excitement. One vehicle closing on another by the right amount. The chaser being hampered by something—losing ground. Regaining ground. We all know about that. . . .

"How long would we have to shoot it?"

"As long as you need. A week should be enough."

"Thank you sir, I'll do my best."

"I know," he smiled as he saw me out of his office.

I returned to my much smaller second assistant's office and picked up the script. I can't remember exactly how it read, but there wasn't much to go on—something like:

> EXT., HOUSE, DAY: Tanith rushes across the lawn jumps into the car. Starts the engine and in a flurry of gravel speeds away. Aware that she is under the evil influence of the unseen Mocata, Rex runs to a second car and begins to give chase.

EXT., COUNTRY ROADS, DAY: Rex chases Tanith. But she is getting away. Spurred on by a supernatural reflection of the beguiling Mocata in the car's rearview mirror.
EXT., SIDE ROAD, DAY: Mocata invokes a cloud of fog. Thereby blinding Rex. Unable to pull up in time, his car hurtles off the road and crashes into a tree.

The above are my words from memory and under no circumstances should they be construed as being the writing of Richard Matheson. (As Jimmy Sangster has observed in the past, we should all have kept copies of the scripts for the films we worked on. But it never occurred to any of us that they would be of archival interest and valuable as documents in their own right, let alone useful for remembrances. A year after a production, they just took up too much space, so they "hit the bin.") Perhaps the sequence was more fully written than I have implied, but certainly not by a great amount. The error the inexperienced screenwriter makes is to go into too much detail, sometimes even including an attempt at establishing camera positions! Avoidance of verbiage is far better, particularly when it comes to action scenes. How could a writer conceivably know the layout of the scenery and imagine the shape of locations or the look of sets that haven't yet been built?

Mind you, I was now set the task of trying to make an exciting two-minute (maximum) mini-film without much structural help. Storyboards were out of the financial equation, as was the input of an editor or anyone else, for that matter. I was on my own and scheduled to start shooting on the following Monday—four days hence. Bert Batt was marvelous, allowing me preparation time away from my current duties with him on the set and offering me considerable encouragement. This was extremely generous of him, as it is certain he would love to have been assigned the task himself, especially as he had already directed second-unit sequences successfully in the past. Actually, if the truth be known, he was far too valuable as the first assistant on the main unit.

I set about doing my own storyboard—and as I can't draw, the pictures were pretty dire and only I could understand them (occasionally). Funny how the memory holds some things more clearly than others. I can see them today, hopeless squiggles in red ink with arrows and an indication of which lens to use.

"Can I have a 150-mm for the Friday?" I asked the production manager, Ian Lewis.

"You'll be lucky."

I explained that even though it was an expensive bit of extra equipment, this lens would be useful to condense the apparent distance between the cars toward the end of the sequence. To my relief, he relented.

The weekend before starting I was consumed with anxiety. Fortunately, Ronnie was back in England and I inveigled him into coming around the locations I planned to use so that he could check out the camera positions with me.

"They're all fine," he said at the end.

"Are you sure I'm not going to cock it up?"

"You won't. Be bold and don't be pushed around."

So I was—probably a bit too much so.

The cameraman-cum-operator assigned to me was a good chap with whom I had worked as an assistant in my post-Beaconsfield, freelance camera days. Dick Bayley had once offered me a permanent assignment as his focus-puller on documentaries. I had declined the offer with some regret, as my goal was drama production.

Monday arrived. The first setup was to see Tanith's car swing around a corner and accelerate down a tree-lined road. Dick positioned the camera in a perfectly acceptable position, but. . . . Well, it just wasn't what I had in mind. I adjusted the framing by tipping the camera up a little to include more sky in the center and the tops of the trees on either side, so as to make them more menacing or oppressive.

"It was all right as it was," said Dick in a slightly miffed tone.

Anyway, we shot it my way.

One of the things about the majority of cameramen is their concern to make well-composed shots, but this may not be what the narrative demands. All that's truly important is the characters, their inner conflict and conflict with others. Back to storytelling again. Furthermore it is essential to know how a scene will be edited; the use of different angles can be smooth if required or jarring, so as to agitate the nerves.

Next camera position: Tanith's car closer, whipping through the frame. Frankly, there is nothing more boring than "up and past" shots of cars, so in an attempt to keep things going, I wanted the camera to move from a medium shot following the car and end up panning with the front

My godfather, Noël Coward, lacking confidence with a baby. My father is second from the left and David Lean is on the right. 1943.

Ronnie takes me through the script of *Oliver Twist*. 1947.

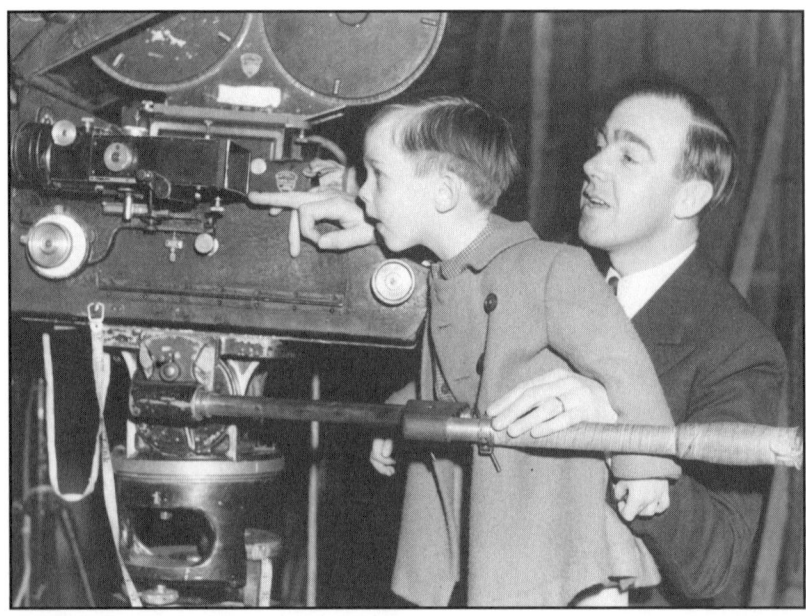
My father gives me instruction on a camera on the set of *Oliver Twist*. 1947.

A Hammer celebration: Anthony Hinds, center, and Anthony Nelson Keys (with a rare glass of wine) beside Peter Cushing, lower left, Bray Studios. 1965.

Terence Fisher (a fine editor) "conducting" on the set of *Dracula—Prince of Darkness*. 1965.

Colonel James Carreras, right, with Christopher Lee, celebrating Hammer's recognition by a Queen's Award to Industry: *Dracula—Prince of Darkness*. 1965.

Anthony Hinds, quietly elegant, although with perhaps a preference for a lower profile than the one he inherited.

Michael Carreras in director's mode.

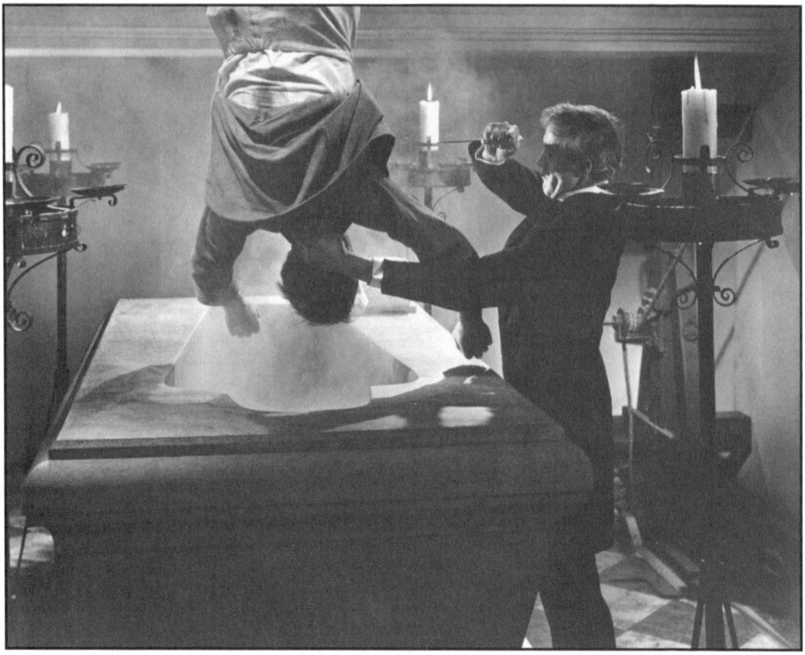

My first experience of bloodletting on Hammer's *Dracula—Prince of Darkness*. 1965.

Waiting for the promised sun. From the left, me (junior camera assistant), Mike Rutter (senior camera assistant), Don Sharp (director), Anthony Nelson Keys, and a half-hidden Arthur Grant. In the background is a section of Dracula's castle, by then revamped into the Winter Palace for *Rasputin—The Mad Monk*. 1965.

Christopher Lee, excellent as Rasputin. 1965.

Joan Fontaine, suitably bloodied and terrified, in a publicity shot for *The Witches*. 1966.

"Parisian" street for *Quatermass and the Pit* at M-G-M, Borehamwood. Roy Baker, center left, with Anthony Nelson Keys. 1967.

Heather and I watch our son being baptized. 1967.

Signed "Bette D.," a publicity shot from *The Anniversary*. 1967.

Bette Davis is at the center, and on either side of her are Jimmy Sangster (left) and Roy Ward Baker (right). Bert Batt is next to Baker. Cameraman Harry Waxman is on the far right, and I am second from the left. On the set of *The Anniversary*. Fourth of July, 1967.

With Bert Batt, right, and another colleague (J. S.), left. 1967.

With actress Kay Walsh as a music-hall performer (Goldilocks) in *Journey to the Unknown*. 1968.

Tony Tenser, right, with whom I worked during a short period away from Hammer; he remains a good friend. On the left is probably the foremost British film censor of all time, John Trevelyan. What he made of Tenser and Hammer beggars belief!

Shane Briant and Gillian Hills in an image that captures the strangeness of the film, *Demons of the Mind*. 1971.

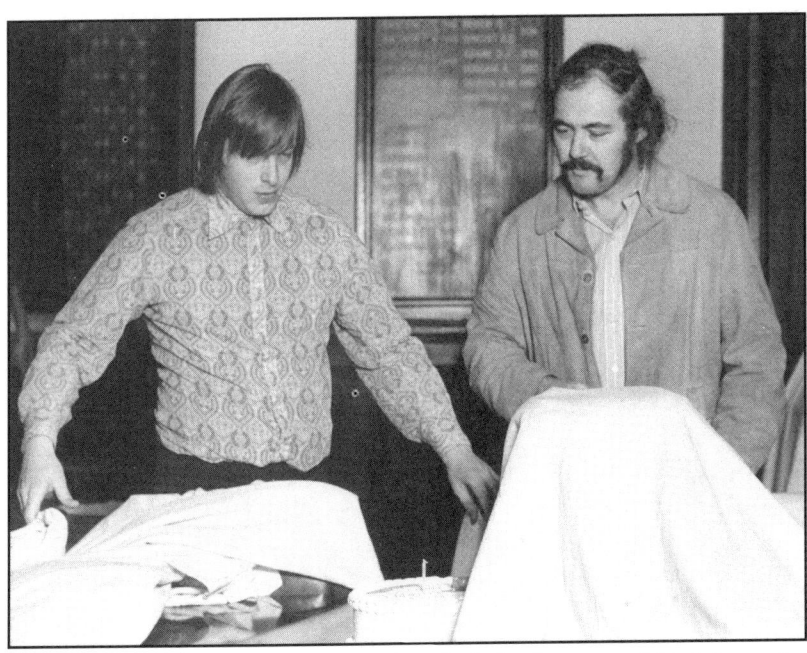

Presenting a bemused Jimmy Sangster with a cake for his forty-seventh birthday, on the set of *Fear in the Night*. 1971.

Jimmy Sangster hugs wardrobe mistress Rosemary Burrows, the unsung heroine: *Fear in the Night*. 1971.

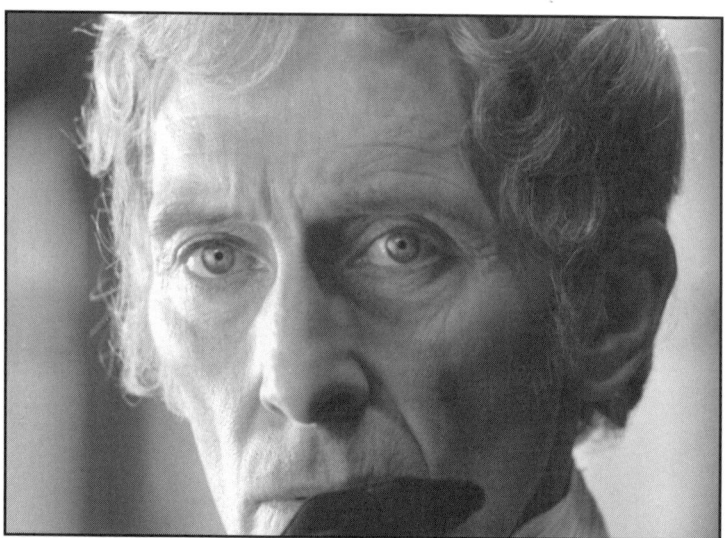

Peter Cushing, with softly curled hair, in *Frankenstein and the Monster from Hell*. 1972.

Roy Skeggs with Terence Fisher (smoking as ever, hospitalization and injured legs notwithstanding) during the filming of *Frankenstein and the Monster from Hell*. 1972.

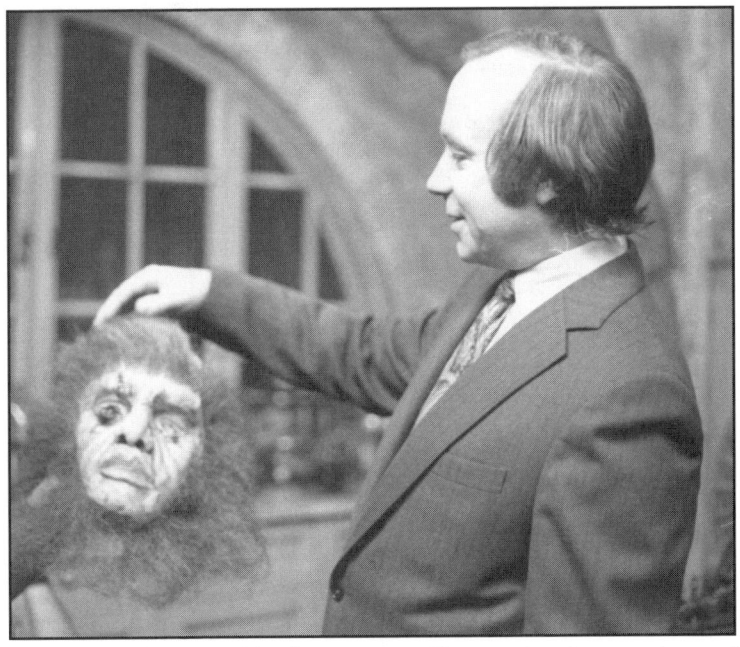

Roy Skeggs with a severed head—an ongoing Hammer situation—on the set of *Frankenstein and the Monster from Hell*. 1972.

Me today.

wheel as it came within an inch of the lens—then leave it to blur out of picture. Potentially this shot might be a bit dangerous, but the period vehicle (with its unfamiliar layout of foot pedals) was driven by a superb film stunt driver called Geoff Silk, looking rather unlike his usual self. He was wearing a costume that went some way toward appearing similar to the one worn by Niké Arrighi—plus a short black wig that was inclined to blow off!

The third shot had Rex's car cornering and spinning into the start of the tree-lined road. This was in the hands of Geoff's brother Jack, an equally expert driver and looking equally odd in a costume matching Leon Greene's. At least he was of a more appropriate build. About ten seconds of screen time was "in the can" by then. So far so good, yet how to sustain the sequence? I had to take a chance.

"Dick, on the next shot on Tanith's car, we must pan up to a close shot of her as she (Geoff) flashes past—and go with her for about a second."

I sensed I was beginning to lose him. "You can't do that."

"Why not?" It was perfectly politely asked; although I was conscious of Ronnie's words about not being pushed around and maybe a certain edge had crept into my voice.

"There's a forty-year-old man in a wig behind the wheel," exclaimed Dick.

"He'll be moving so fast that no one will be able to tell." And if they do, I thought, we wouldn't use the shot—but it was worth the try.

By midday we had four setups completed.

After lunch there was another difference of opinion with a similar close shot on Rex flying past.

By now I knew that Dick was getting fed up with this upstart who had once been his assistant, so it wasn't a surprise to me when I got back to the studio in the evening to hear he'd already telephoned Ian Lewis and asked to be released from the assignment.

The following morning I was in trouble again, this time with the editors. It was imperative for me to see my rushes to satisfy myself that we could go into close shots on the Silk brothers. At 7:00 A.M. there was no one in the cutting rooms, so I picked up the editors' key from the studio gate and the cans of film already back from Technicolor. I laced up the Moviola and started running through the footage. I really shouldn't have done it, because I was far too inexperienced to run properly this clattering piece of viewing equipment that looked like an alien robot in a sci-fi film produced in the nineteen-thirties. *Clatter-clatter-clatter-graunch*—the film came off the rails and a great section spewed out all over the floor. Was my material really destined for the cutting room floor?

Try again. . . . A bit more successful this time, I got through the first two shots. *Clatter-clatter-clatter. . .* music to my ears . . . *graunch*. More film on the floor, and this time with perforations where there shouldn't have been. Once the situation was recovered, I ground on with not much time to spare—due on the location, fifteen miles away, at 8:00 A.M. Then up came the shot: perfect. With the speed of it, Geoff Silk looked exactly like our heroine.

That's how the wrath of the editors was incurred—me messing up their rushes. Never mind, it had to be done. Without knowing we'd be safe to go in even tighter on the drivers' faces, we'd have had a bit of a wasted day (contact with the studio from a location in the countryside was out of the question before mobile phones).

Emboldened by knowing what could be achieved, we had a good day, and the new cameraman was great. Cars tore blindly through the instant blanket of fog called down by Mocata and created in reality by Les Bowie, who provided us with an extraordinary piece of equipment called something like "Bezzlar." Volumes of smoke filled the screen, and so long as the machine was placed upwind it worked well. But with the capricious breezes of England, the position of this wheel-mounted device had to be changed constantly.

Bert came up with a very good suggestion for a shot. Attach an Arriflex camera (under-cranked to make the action appear faster on screen) to the running board of Rex's Lancia with the front wheel big in the foreground and chase Tanith down a very windy road. Complicated. It would have to be filmed in one take over a distance of about a mile, so we could keep cutting back to it as the gap closes. A pretty lane, which was used infrequently, was found in Buckinghamshire. Nevertheless, any traffic that might happen along would have to be stopped at the far end; anything behind us didn't matter. Even basic walkie-talkies were not then in use in the film industry, so someone had to drive down to instruct the assistant to close the road at the far end and then hurry back to give us the all clear.

Off we went, with the cameraman and me in the back seat and his assistant in the front left, as Jack Silk chased after Geoff. Swinging left as the car went sharply to the right—the front wheel briefly covering the camera's view of the car ahead . . . a swing the other way . . . straight and then another swing. All went well and we didn't meet another car.

In case there might have been a camera problem or something else that was not quite right, it was decided to do a second take with a fresh roll of film in a different magazine.

Back to the top. Given the all clear. Run the camera. And off we went.

Left . . . right . . . ahead . . . right. . . . Actually it should have been right, but just as Jack was about to spin the wheel, a tire burst and we went straight on, leapt a ditch, and landed in some undergrowth.

A moment or two of utter silence—then:

"Is everyone all right?" I asked in a shaky voice.

Thank God they were, but the camera wasn't very well. The side of the magazine had sheered off and film was unspooling into the ditch, its mount had been ripped away and the film transportation system looked like it shouldn't!

And the whole front of the car was smashed in.

The upside was that the first take was securely in the can. The downside—no camera and no car and it wasn't even lunchtime.

Back to the studio to report the mishap to Mr. Keys. He was sanguine enough. No one had been hurt, which was the main thing.

New orders—we were to go out the next day to film traveling-matte plates (blue screen or process work) to be used as the background for studio close-up shots of the principals in the chase. This would require a special camera with rock-steady register pins to hold each frame firmly in place as it was exposed. With the camera securely bolted down, the net result would be a shot without any drifting, impossible with an Arriflex I had always been told, as it is bereft of the essential pins. This seemed a bit silly to me. All secure and steady and then we'd trundle along the road and that's when the image became naturally unsteady as tires rolled over tarmac. It wasn't for me to reason why.

Without prior knowledge of how long or where a plate is to be used in the final version of the film, it is necessary for it (the plate) to run for as long as possible without interruption. Prolonging the plate for a period movie was not easy, considering the pylons and other modern paraphernalia littering the countryside. Fortunately we found a longish spot of road that was in the clear, and ABPC's prized high-speed

Mitchell effects camera was taken out of its case and placed on a well-anchored tripod on the rear platform of a camera car. We did well enough and had got all we could out of this location looking backwards. Only a forward angle remained. Terry had requested this especially for one section in the sequence where Tanith glances back to see Rex chasing behind her.

Gently the camera car moved off to take us to the starting position. Then, as if in slow motion, the tripod began to give way . . . tilting forward . . . its front leg breaking . . . the camera toppling to the road and getting itself run over.

At least Terry had that chuckle about it an hour later when we met in the men's room.

The second unit was now altogether out of work. Actually not out of work, but out of equipment.

"There's only one thing for it," sighed Mr. Keys. "You'll have to get on with the third unit." He smiled and added, "None of it was your fault at all."

I thanked him as I left to return home for an early night.

One of the tensest sequences in the film has Tanith and all the good guys, led by the Duc de Richleau, in the middle of a chalk circle in a large room. This way they will remain protected from the fatal visitation of Satan's messenger. A winged black horse enters, and on its back is an armoured rider, his face hidden by chain mail. If our characters ever see his face, they will die. The horse rears up and the messenger reaches for his mask . . . is about to pull it off . . . *cut.*

That's all my bit was.

With the repaired Arriflex camera in place and the horse harnessed with its wings, everything was set. Red shooting light illuminated outside the stage. Roll the camera. . . .

"Action!"

In comes the horse—hold for a moment; then:

"Horse up. . . ." I called.

The stunt rider pulled it up perfectly—slowly, menacingly. . . .

"Hand. . . ."

His gauntleted hand reached for the chain mail. Two and a half seconds. . . . And. . . . and the wings fell off the horse without warning. The metal harness just collapsed from the stress put on it as the horse reared.

"Could someone please ask Mr. Keys if he would kindly come to the stage?" I asked.

I went back to being a reasonably efficient second assistant for a fortnight while all the damage was being been repaired, and then we were once again able to carry on with the second-unit work as well as the third. All fine. But it had taken a total of three weeks to shoot what amounted to under two minutes of screen time. Directors, I mean proper directors, are invariably opposed to second-unit material; if only time and budget could ever allow it, they'd always prefer to do their own stuff. Given the situation, Terry was generous about my efforts.

I can make no claim to being even remotely brilliant, but the first sign of a hidden something that has proved an invaluable asset throughout my career, and life in general, brought itself to my attention when we started work on the major sequence at the end of the film. It featured a Satanic gathering (including a man/goat character played by Eddie Powell) in the dark woods of familiar Black Park at night. The entire cast was on call for the sequence, plus some additional actors playing Satanists—not extras but Equity professionals, because they were to speak lines. They weren't given character names but were identified by very basic Satanist 1, Satanist 2, and so on. As there was a shortage of changing facilities on the location, these additional cast members would have to share three caravans. I decided to put John Faulkener, Richard Scott, and Bert Vivian together in one. All very British; no mixed sexes in those times of propriety. Moments before allocating the facility, a doubt nudged my brain. I called the casting director.

"Irene, this Bert Vivian. Is it a man or woman?"

"A woman."

Great! How was I to know this from a "Casting Advice Memo"?

"Might have guessed! *Ciao*...."

I wondered why, and still wonder why, a bell registered in my head. On this occasion a minor *faux pas* over dressing facilities could easily have been put right, but this little bell was to ring later in life and forewarn me of the more dangerous waters. Thank God for it.

Filming after dark on the beach of a South Pacific island sounds like quite good fun, but otherwise night shooting is very tedious. As one sets off for work, one sees, with envy, cars on the other side of the road bearing their occupants home—most likely. And by now, in late summer, the nights were getting longer. All very busy—lots of people to get to lots of different positions, playback tracks for witches to dance to, trying to keep everyone warm and awake. Truly our third assistant and I were run off our feet. Still, there was a decent cooked breakfast to look forward to at 7:00 A.M. All went smoothly enough, and by the end of the fourth night, the picture was finished. Then came the accident—one I am grateful not to have witnessed.

Terry was well known to enjoy a scotch or three, and shortly after we wrapped, he enjoyed a few more on top. On leaving a London pub, he started across a side street and was hit a mighty broadside by a speeding vehicle. Poor man was terribly shaken up, in a lot of pain and in plaster for many weeks.

They say lightning never strikes twice. But they, whoever they are, are not always right.

· 7 ·

Egg and Chips

I moved her up against the wall, her body melting into mine as I kissed her long and hard. The stuff dreams are made of—well, nearly.

"Cut."

And that was that.

Bert Batt and I had finished our 1967 stint with Hammer and, with another film in between, early the following year we were away in Ireland doing a picture for Columbia called *Lock Up Your Daughters!* based on a successful stage musical. It had great promise but was ultimately a disappointing eighteenth-century romp of the *Tom Jones* type. Madness—the producers cut the songs. The opening scene shows love-hungry sailors arriving ashore after a long voyage and out to get any woman they can. Plenty of extras kissing plenty of willing girls. Since we were away from London's union-controlled Central Casting, we could use nonunion members, and I'd already picked various people from our crew to take part. When cameraman Peter Suschitzky demurred, I tried to persuade him by saying "I'd do it myself for two pins." The director, Peter Coe, overheard me and said, "Done." So off I went to the wardrobe department to be kitted out as a "tar," with a pigtail and all, and then back on the set, in front of the camera, to kiss a very pretty colleen. Many years later, when I was producing *The Irish R.M.*, I was to meet Sue Dineen again, and we laughingly recalled our two kisses (two takes) and agreed, under the circumstances, it had been legitimate enough for a young married man to behave in such a way.

Dinner at the hotel that evening: Bert, me, and our third assistant—and Anthony Nelson Keys. This was not a Hammer production, and, like us, he had taken on an assignment for a different company, this time as associate producer to the successful David Deutsch. Another Hammer person on the film was Michael Carreras's son Chris. He was just starting out on his career, representing his family's fourth generation in films—rare for such a new industry.

Coming along on the location with ANK was his wife Maggie, and over several weeks I got to know them both very, very well. By now I had earned enough stripes to drop the "Sir" and call him Tony. Clearly I remember enjoying a most succulent steak, more than liberally sprinkled with garlic, and him telling me how he had no taste for garlic, and going on to say he really wasn't very keen on food at all, simply eating as a necessity. What with Bert's dislike of alcohol and Tony's dislike of culinary niceties, I might have found myself in the company of Philistines had it not been for Maggie. A loving wife, elegant, very soft-spoken, well educated, and naturally intelligent, she had the kind of attractive laughter that makes one smile automatically. (Useful trick she taught me—always run the hot water into an old-fashioned bath to a height of about two inches and leave it to heat up the bottom for a while before adding the rest. She drew a bath for ANK every evening in such a way. Location shooting allows you to learn so much more about your colleagues than in a day-by-day environment! And yes, I was still wearing paper underpants.)

Coffee arrived and my mentor sat back in his chair and lit a cigarette.

Exhaling, he said in a pleased voice, "I've had a call from Tony Hinds. They want another *Frankenstein*."

"For when?' Bert asked.

"Next year. I've got to come up with a story."

On set the next day, Bert and I were playing with a golf ball. This occupation kept us amused while waiting for camera tracks to be laid or lamps to be positioned. One of us would throw it down onto hard ground—bounce—and the other caught it. All very puerile. It was his turn, but he hesitated and then handed the ball back to me as Tony Keys approached.

"About *Frankenstein*," said Bert.

"Good news, isn't it?" Tony replied, still very pleased at the idea of getting back to his old ways. That morning he was clearly much happier than he had been since the start of this production. He felt he'd been excluded from the top echelon and had to fight to get every piece of information he needed to do his job half decently.

"Who's going to write it?" Bert asked.

"We don't know yet—not Tony Hinds apparently. And Michael's off doing other things."

"I'd like to have a go," Bert stated.

Tony pursed his lips. "We need the story first."

"We can get on with it here in the evenings."

So that is what happened: They started developing *Frankenstein Must Be Destroyed* in a hotel room in Kilkenny.

A week later Bert received a letter from Tony Hinds asking if he would like to be the first assistant director on the TV series Hammer was going to make for Twentieth Century Fox later in the year. Bert declined, his heart now set on getting on with his script. Tony H. wrote to Bert again and this time enquired whether he thought I was ready to handle the job in his stead.

"What I'd really like to do," I told Bert, "is to become a unit production manager."

Very kindly he wrote back to Tony Hinds with the suggestion. Shortly I received news that I should report for an interview in London as soon as the current film wrapped. My time in Ireland was pretty good fun, all things considered—an important principal cast and hundreds of extras. Nevertheless I raced eagerly to the airport after the last shot and was back home with my wife and little son before the sun went down.

Heather was by now about seven months pregnant with our second child, and although I had preferred the idea of a daughter the first time around, I was now completely hooked on being the father of a little boy and hoped for another. Not that it mattered remotely so long as they were both healthy.

Within forty-eight hours of my return, I was sitting in Tony Hinds' office. I'd met him many times before, but now I was about to know him much better—and what a pleasure it was to be. Sad to say, this was not the case with the other man present. He was the senior production manager on the series and should have had confidence in his role, but he carried two large chips on both of his shoulders.

Journey to the Unknown is an anthology of seventeen films about weird goings-on—not exactly normal Hammer fare, though not far off it. There was good and bad about the fact that they were unconnected pieces. Good, because the same actors would never cross over episodes and nor would the sets; therefore any number of films could be made concurrently. In theory, with a schedule of ten days' shooting on each, the whole series could have been completed in just two weeks. Impossible, though—not enough crews in the U.K. and not enough stage space. What we did was to have two main units—A and B—each making eight films apiece over a period of sixteen weeks with an entirely separate crew to shoot one independently. It was tight, but we could just make the U.S. air dates (to commence in September 1968 on the ABC network), even though the last of the episodes would still be shooting at the time. The bad side of an anthology was (and indeed still is) that, because there was no actor continuity, audiences lacked "unmissable" characters to watch each week. In the end it's what crippled the show—having said as much, I must add that the films still play on television today.

M-G-M—"the studio up the road" from ABPC—was to be our base and I for one was happy to go back there as the unit manager on the B unit. While we were moving into our offices, the Hollywood executive producer arrived. Joan Harrison had been Alfred Hitchcock's script assistant in England, and when he went to America in 1939 he had taken her with him. They were not lovers (as far as I know); Joan was simply an essential part of a good team. Subsequently she married the prolific novelist Eric Ambler. Her credits are numerous, but she is probably best remembered as the principal producer of the long-running fifties and sixties TV series *The Hitchcock Hour*. Because of a professional relationship with her husband, my father and my mother, Beryl, had met her while in America, and the four had become good friends. I didn't know this when we started at M-G-M, and she never said anything to me (nor did my parents); she cleverly let me stand on my own feet. In later years we became close in our own right. The most important thing to say here about this new executive in the Hammer fold is she was entirely different from any other I encountered. Soignée in a word. Miss Harrison had a special quality that defies automatic attribution by gender. She knew her job inside and out, was a fine critic of her own work, and had an air of quiet confidence. Not for a moment was she defensive and not for a moment aggressive about being a woman in a male-dominated field. Such a wonderful example she was, then and now. Coming along with her, as an associate, was Jack Fleischmann, a great big, bearded, bear of a man with a winning smile. That tragedy was to befall him before the completion of production is one of those moments in life that cannot be forgotten.

Also moving into the offices was Tony Hinds, who was harbouring some grief about the situation. As he had understood it, Miss Harrison and Jack were to have been the producers, and he the executive producer—meaning he could be more "hands-off." This was not the way it was seen by anyone else. "Producer" was his title. Fortunately a nontitular compromise was reached. Tony would be at the studio first thing in the morning and would be able to leave in the early afternoon. The other two would be in by ten and stay until the end of the day.

This did not keep Tony from approving locations, and I recall on one occasion visiting a manor house with him and a director. We piled out of the studio's administration building and into his car—an elegant blue Bentley, with a chauffeur, and the chauffeur's dog (a white poodle). Sensing my place, I started to get into the front, while Tony and the director opened the rear doors.

"Oh no, Chris, sit in the back." Apparently the dog was assigned the front passenger seat, and we all squashed together behind it (despite the impression associated with the name, these aren't big cars inside).

The location approved, the director and I were dropped off at the main gate of M-G-M and Tony headed home.

Some explanation is needed about this and other incidents involving Tony Hinds. He never enjoyed the actual process of making films. Usually his desk was remarkably clear of any littering pieces of paper, and it showed not the remotest sign of any of the fiscal matters a producer must deal with. On asking him how he could be certain the weekly checks he was signing were correct, his reply was that the accountants had to be relied upon. Apparently he wasn't very interested in keeping a double-checking eye on them—nor should he have been, actually, because instinctively and by experience he would have known well enough what things cost.

His was a role in life brought about because of his father. Will Hinds had been the heir to Hinds Jewellers, a very prosperous chain in the UK, but his heart had lain elsewhere—comedy vaudeville. Often acts would be two-handers, and he had an equally ambitious partner. Together they started the quest for a joint stage name. Some time before, another vaudevillian had selected one for himself that came to him while traveling in a railway carriage—"Nosmo King." Our two took the same tack. Walking down a London street, they observed the plaque on the wall, "Hammersmith Broadway." They duly became "Hammer and Smith." Subsequently Will Hammer became involved in film distribution and, in due course, production, along with Enrico Carreras for their Exclusive Films. Later the name was changed to Hammer Films. (For some unknown reason I still have in my possession a blank sheet of Exclusive's notepaper.)

On leaving the army, Tony Hinds had wanted to take up writing as a career, but he was sort of obliged to join the family firm. In the end it might have been harmful, as it hampered his literary ambitions. Nevertheless, his avoidance of confrontation aside, he became an extremely good producer—and I feel qualified to make this statement because I served under him.

With shooting soon under way, I grew daily more aware of the chips weighing so heavily on our senior production manager's shoulders. His qualifications for the job were sound enough, but he had seen his peers advance beyond him. There is probably no reason why he should have been left behind; it was just one of those things—perhaps, simply, he had not been in the right place at the right time, or perhaps he suffered from chronic self-doubt. I'm not going to try to analyze the situation; however, he was evidently jealous of his junior managers. We were on a path that potentially led upward and he was on the way back, having never really climbed the heights. The adage, "Be kind to people on the way up because you might need them on the way down," was fixed clearly in my mind from the outset, and I can truthfully say I was kind to him. The reverse did not apply—no doubt exacerbated by the successful career of my father, who was a contemporary. Furthermore, I suspect he held me in some disdain because I was a pretty regular employee of Hammer and not a crewmember of his own choosing. Unfortunately, one could see his decline as, earlier and earlier in the day, he would inform us he was "off to check the studio's alternators" (electrical generators)—his code word for a drink in the bar. His alcoholic forays resulted in his finding fault with our work. In the end he did not contribute a great deal to the production, and, although the possessor of a good sense of humor, he was a soul who had lost his way. It is only fair to add that there were those who admired his ability—more is the pity I cannot be counted among them.

July 16th, 1968: Shuna Neame was born—my second child to arrive while I was "resident" at M-G-M. This time the call from the Irish voice at the nursing home came through while I was in a dubbing theater taking instruction from the editors on re-recording voice tracks (looping or ADR). Another round of applause. A short while later, on seeing my daughter, I felt extreme contentment; gone was the urge for a second little boy. I was the father of a beautiful little girl.

A Tuesday, two weeks later: Roy Ward Baker came into my office three and a half days before he was due to finish his ten-day schedule on one of the episodes.

"We're coming in under."

Oh, my God. A nightmare situation. Contractually each of the films had to have a running length of a "television hour." Although prescribed exactly, it wasn't exactly exact! The U.S. hour (for Twentieth / ABC) was forty-eight minutes "on the button"; the U.K. hour (a market we had to consider contractually as well), needed between fifty and fifty-two minutes. A further complication related to the U.S. / U.K. transmission speed of twenty-four camera frames per second and twenty-five in Britain (where, *ipso facto*, the films would run for less screen time). That's enough of the technicalities, other than to say that a movie that runs on television for two hours in America will have a running time on the BBC of around one hour and fifty-five minutes. The most acute ears will notice the resultant slight change in vocal and musical pitch throughout.

We could usually handle the length issue, and a film coming "off the floor" a little over was invariably best and easy to tighten. But if it was under length, there was nowhere to go.

Putting on a brave face, I asked Roy by how much we were short.

"According to Estelle, four minutes."

Estelle Stewart was the continuity girl (as script supervisors were then called) and she had a reputation for accurately assessing the edited timing of what had already been shot, as well as foreseeing that which was yet to be filmed. She had to be taken very seriously.

It was a lousy time of day to get this information. My immediate superior was off "checking the alternators," Tony Hinds was on a location survey with the manager of A unit, and Miss Harrison and Jack Fleischmann were in the screening room viewing rushes and were strictly uninterruptible. With the amount of footage being delivered daily by two shooting crews and double the normal amount of edited material to see, they were likely to be unavailable for several hours. First back was the production manager, who tossed the ball back into my court. The next one due was Tony, but he went straight on home after his survey. So I had to wait.

Eventually I was able to explain the problem to Miss Harrison, who assured me she would telephone the writer, Robert Bloch, in America and get him to write an extra scene involving only those actors still under contract and one of the studio sets still standing. He was a quick worker, and if everyone pulled their fingers out, the new pages could be couriered to England and, thanks to time zones, arrive astonishingly rapidly by noon the next day—this was before the advent of fax machines.

Nothing came.

Joan Harrison was puzzled and so tried again.

Thursday—still nothing.

I was never to discover what went amiss.

Something had to be done urgently, so I got out my pen and started writing. A few years before, and like just about everyone else who has anything to do with movies, I had tried my hand at a screenplay. (It's still at the bottom of some drawer or other.) By Friday only two actors would be on call and only one small set available. Four minutes of screen time and about four hours to shoot it in. The constraints were a good thing; they always are, as it necessitates very creative thinking. An hour later and my scene was written. I presented it to Miss Harrison, who gave her approval. Approval was also required from Tony Hinds on behalf of Hammer. Quite understandably, as a writer himself, he did a bit of tinkering. The thing I learned—and it has proved to be very useful throughout my career—is that, given this kind of situation, you take the story off sideways for the required duration and get it back in line by the end of the scene. In a way it is a mini-film in its own right.

Shooting got under way after lunch on the Friday and by the evening the episode was up to length and completed on schedule.

What a wonderful moment to see the result of my endeavour on screen during Monday's rushes. The writing was just about passable, but the scene was excellent. How could it have been otherwise? The two actors playing together were the superb Catherine Lacey and American actress, Julie Harris, who, a few years before, had starred in *I Am a Camera* as Sally Bowles. The added bonus was that I had penned a small part of a script written by the renowned writer of *Psycho*.

There was no payment made for this extracurricular work, nor should there have been, and anyway my father had brought me up to believe one should always do more than is asked of one. It was therefore a great surprise when Jack Fleischmann and Miss Harrison presented me with a gift for my newborn daughter—a beautiful silver-backed hairbrush.

A few months later Joan would attend her christening, and a few months later Jack would be dead. He had been diagnosed as suffering from Hodgkin's disease and returned to the States for unsuccessful treatment while we were still shooting *Journey to the Unknown*.

The charming Norman Lloyd came to England in his place, and for the last couple of episodes, he took over from Joan as executive producer (because of farcical tax laws she could only remain in England for a limited period). Norman had started out as an actor in the 1930s, soon joining Orson Welles's Mercury Theatre. Later came films, including Hitchcock's *Saboteur*, in which he is to be seen falling to his apparent death from the Statue of Liberty. His work with the great director brought about his teaming with Joan Harrison as an associate producer on *Alfred Hitchcock Presents*. When it came time for Norman to take the reins, he did so smoothly and was a very good boss indeed.

In addition to the aforementioned actresses, there were many fairly well known names in the cast, an absolute requirement of ABC Television. As with all TV series, the casting of these principal actors was most often very near to the deadline. Once they were picked, work permits had to be acquired for those from the United States and everyone was given a medical examination for insurance purposes. God knows what would have happened if the prognosis of any of them was death within a week!

Among them was the incomparable Joseph Cotten. Imagine, if you will, a twenty-five-year-old negotiating petty cash with the man who'd played Holly Martins in *The Third Man*. He had insisted on wearing his own clothes for the episode, which, although a little out of style, were probably good for the character, and one suit had been damaged beyond repair. He was pointed in my direction to seek compensation.

"How much!" I exclaimed from behind a desk that was far too large for my taste.

He repeated the figure—around twice my weekly salary! I'm ashamed to say I beat him down by 30 percent or so. He wasn't a rich man, as far as I know, and here was a youngster, admittedly doing what he was supposed to do on a Hammer production, but at the end of it I felt I'd been a bit unfair to a man who was always polite. *Mea culpa.*

Joe's suit had become damaged during the filming of a train crash scene and his escape from the wreckage. The design of the sequence required a great deal of creative rethinking, as what we were trying to show was:

> EXT., RAILWAY TRACK, DAY: A commuter train speeds past CAMERA.
> INT., RAILWAY CARRIAGE, DAY: Our character is reading the evening newspaper.
> EXT., RAILWAY, DAY: The train jumps the tracks and hurtles on for several hundred yards before toppling on its side.
> INT., WRECKED RAILWAY CARRIAGE, DAY: Our character disentangles himself from the debris and starts to scramble out.
> EXT., RAILWAY, DAY: He stumbles away from the scene.

As before, the above wording is my own from memory—not the screenwriter's pen.

I cannot for the life of me think why someone more senior to me did not handle the situation, but there I was again, trying to figure out how to achieve something that didn't fit the budget prepared by Hammer's in-house accountant, Roy Skeggs. My task was simply to work out the shooting schedule, and it couldn't have been done without knowing how the sequence would be shot. In response to the query put to the director, he said, "What do you suggest?'

"There's a large railway shunting yard not far off, but I doubt we'll get permission to shoot there. The best bet, in my opinion, is to make it a night sequence for a start. Businessmen usually return home after dark, unless it's midsummer. That way we won't be able to see beyond a hundred yards—a hundred feet, as far as film is concerned."

We fiddled the idea around for a while and opted to shoot in the studio (during the day, naturally) and place a strewn train carriage at one side of a stage with an avalanche of balsa wood debris crashing down. Then we'd fill the space with smoke generated by our potty-professor Les Bowie's arcane Bezzlar machine. Finally, because of the time it would take to film, we decided a second-unit crew should shoot the sequence, with the director giving last-minute instructions when called over from another stage.

Back to the opening of the scene, the easy bit: Train rushing through the darkness—to be grabbed on any nearby location that was sufficiently illuminated. Then to the inside of the carriage—Joe Cotten seated there on an elastic mounted deck, with carriage-like walls, reading his newspaper. And then on cue, throw the handheld camera around a bit, with a violent lurch backwards by the actor . . . sounds of ripping metal . . . splitting wood . . . screams. . . .

And *cut to*: Darkness . . . brightening . . . tumbling bodies . . . and Joe getting away. . . .

The cinematographer of B unit, Ken Talbot, a smallish, silver-haired man with a pleasant and confident nature, suggested his own camera operator should photograph the second-unit work. Moray Grant and I had become great friends since our *Frankenstein Created Woman* days and regularly traveled to work in one car on this production.

"Would you like to photograph the rail crash?" I asked him on our way back to our homes that evening. He gave me the answer I'd expected. This was to be the start of a good long-time working relationship, as later on he joined me as cinematographer in his own right on some pictures away from Hammer.

He filmed the train wreck very well and did something I thought rather clever by including the flashing red shooting light at the side of the stage in the picture. It gave the scene an added bit of atmosphere. Once all the shots had been put together in the cutting room, we knew we'd done a good job: a totally convincing sequence.

Summer was giving way to autumn, and the end was in sight. That was when the B unit crew (the one I was responsible for) started to get a bit rebellious. We were filming for five days at a location forty miles away from the studio—a journey on standard roads of about an hour and a half each way each day. Perhaps we could have found somewhere closer to base, but nothing quite as good as Frensham Ponds. I had known this lovely spot since childhood, and it was just right. Our senior production manager, who had shot there before out of nearby Shepperton, suggested it—he wasn't all bad—but the decision to go ahead presented me with a problem. The cause was the traditional British Studios' failure to play fair with crews when it came to overtime. In America you could go where you liked and for as long as you liked so long as you were prepared to pay for it. Not so for us.

On a television series, it is absolutely essential to keep on schedule. Various tactics can be employed to safeguard that in most areas, including under-length episodes and "unrest"—although the treatment for the latter I employed for the current situation was an unapproved method and very much thought of by my peers as being "not cricket." To hell with it, something had to be done. Quickly I went over to the accounts department and asked them to give me three hundred pounds—a great deal of money then. The assistant accountant was commendably brave and handed it over.

"Where do I sign?"

"Sign later."

He was being sensible—obviously no one who intends to make any business his life's career is going to pocket the company's funds! Except, extraordinarily, three years on, this young man happened to do just that.

I jumped into my car and headed for the location—the knight in shining armor who was about to save the day by handing out greenbacks to a flagging crew. Twenty-five miles later and my car went *clunk . . . zlunk . . . phhhut. . . .* And I was sitting at the roadside with more egg on my face than an ostrich could produce in the mating season. I mean there I was with hordes of lolly and with no apparent way of arriving on the location to dispense it before the disgruntled crew beat their weary way home. Drop mobile phones from the equation and drop an instant rescue team. A house a hundred yards away offered some sort of a lifeline, and the most helpful lady there allowed me to use her phone. I managed to contact a friend from childhood, who lived nearby and worked from home.

He saved the situation by hurrying me to the location, getting there just in time to hear the assistant director call, "It's a wrap." What a pity the actual director was not a bit more grateful for my efforts—he had been the one to push the crew to their limits, and without this little gratuity they would inevitably have "worked to rule" and in so doing taken away a third of his subsequent shooting days.

The ongoing struggle to keep the show on schedule was probably the major thrust required of the unit manager, and I was forever trying to come up with ideas to achieve this goal. The worst one, for which I rightly received an admonishment from Ronnie, my father, when I later told him of my cleverness, was when I intentionally arranged to park a noisy generator within perfect earshot of the microphones, thereby stopping the rather fussy sound recordist from demanding an extra time-consuming "take" for his department. They could re-voice later, I glibly thought. But what of performance, the disembodiment? I hadn't taken this into account. *Mea culpa* again, but it was all part of learning.

A great deal of bad press was going around the industry during the sixties, seventies, and early eighties about the restrictive practices of the unions. Whereas this was justified criticism in many respects, there are always two sides to a coin. Traditionally the owners and managers of businesses had the whip hand, and it was only in the early part of the twentieth century that workers found their voice and managed to swing the pendulum the other way—so much so that the tail was soon wagging the dog. Man-hours galore were wasted as arguments were put up by one side and countered by the other. Eternally I shall be grateful to my father for insisting that I start at the very bottom of the industry, because it allowed me to see where the workers' grievances could come from, and by now, as a manager, how the needs of a production might readily cause conflict and why a fine line had to be trod. I was about to witness a complete reversal of the usual process.

Director Don Chaffey, who looked as if he should have been a pirate, with his colorful cravats and pointed beard (an earring would have suited him well), was to do a very good episode, which spanned several years. The main set was the lobby of a seaside hotel. The first sequences, from an earlier and more opulent period, would take two days to complete—finishing on a Tuesday evening. The always clever art director, Roy Stannard (with whom I have been privileged to work on many subsequent occasions), and his team then had to re-dress the set to a dilapidated state of cobwebs and peeling wallpaper for filming on the Wednesday afternoon. After that they had the Thursday to alter it yet again to another period for filming on the

Friday. And finally their task was to bring it up to date and looking very different from anything before by the following Monday. For this the construction crew would need to work over the weekend.

Old Bluey Hill was the first assistant director, still full of good humor and gin, and he kept the shooting crew on target. The construction crew were the ones with the problem. By 4:30 P.M. on the Thursday, it was clear the revamping of the set would not be completed on time, and that meant no shooting on Friday, and that meant no re-dressing over the weekend, and that meant we were in big trouble.

"It's not going to be ready," Harry, the studio's head shop steward, said, stating the only too obvious.

"No," I replied despondently.

"What are you going to do?"

"No idea. What do you suggest?"

"I could always tell the men they'll have to work straight through the night."

"Twenty hours nonstop? But it's against your own rules, Harry."

"Depends on how you interpret them. Anyway I wrote most of them. Want me to fix it?"

"God, yes."

"You'll have to pay them triple time."

It would assuredly be far, far cheaper than having no set to film on.

"Done," I said.

"Leave it with me."

The set was ready shortly before midnight—obviously there had been some high-speed work! But I was happy as I drove home and crashed out for a few hours. What was and is still interesting is that Harry had chucked away the union agreement to fit the situation, and I had been lucky enough to be able to sanction payment on behalf of the absent studio management. If formally approached, they would have declined the union's offer to bail us out of a difficulty, which could have caused us untold damage because it threatened good old "custom and practice." What an unadventurous world!

This incident raises a serious issue about autonomy in the film industry in the twenty-first century. Thirty-odd years ago, and even as a simple unit manager, I was left alone to deal with matters as I saw fit. If I made the wrong decision there'd be trouble from on high. If I was lucky and made the right one, no more was heard of it. As financing is arranged now, a film is often funded by several companies and each of their head men or women demands recognition as a producer—which usually they are pitifully far from being—and each demands that his or her approval be sought before virtually any decision is made. Worse still, there are the sidekicks, who are benignly permitted to give their mostly rubbishy input, and my God, they seem to be able to produce forests worth of paperwork about nothing. Poor misguided souls. Too many "injuns." Catastrophic. Think about a Boeing 747 crossing the Atlantic with eight captains having a go at the controls and you can picture the incompetence rife in the film and television industry today.

Kay Walsh played one of the principals in Don Chaffey's episode. Her character was a widowed ex-music-hall actress, who had appeared on stage since childhood with the boy who became her husband. Around the walls of her home were many photographs of her earlier years, invariably with her by now deceased spouse. Who could I find to depict him?

"Anthony Nelson Keys," I suggested to Tony Hinds. "He's got the right sort of cheeky face."

"Good idea."

"Will you ask him?"

"No, you can deal with it."

"I couldn't possibly."

"You'll have to," he told me as he slipped a book into his briefcase and left for the day.

It was Maggie Keys who answered the phone and, taking advantage of someone who had become a friend in Ireland, I pitched the idea to her, adding that as Tony's father, "Bunch," had trod the boards, it was apposite. She concurred and said she'd get Tony to call me back when he returned from a game of golf.

An hour later: "Very well, young man. Where do you want me? And when?"

I gave him the relevant details. "And we'll costume you as various characters—a clown; a ringmaster, Burlington Bertie, Harry Lauder and. . . ."

He took to the idea but added, "I draw the line at Little Lord Fauntleroy."

Two days later we had our pictures, with my (hopefully temporary) ex-boss dressed in various outrageous costumes and, for one shot, sitting on the lap of Kay Walsh, who was made up with rosy cheeks like pompoms. A lot of fun was had that day. As I wiped away my tears of laughter, she said, as both of them dried theirs, "We'll get our own back on you for this one day, Kitty-kar."

Neither of them did. But Tony, without a trace of malice, was to give me some hard times ahead.

By the middle of autumn 1968, the series was complete and with its finale came a surprising statement. "I'm retiring,"
"What?"
"I'm retiring," repeated Tony Hinds.
"Why?"
"I've had enough."

He was only forty-six and it didn't seem plausible. It is said that he left the industry in disgust because Joan Harrison took the senior role on this show. I don't really think it was as simple as that. Film had never really been the world for him; he'd been born into it and had been prevented from going his own way.
"You'll be back."
"No," he replied.
"Within a year," I predicted. "And I'll bet you ten pounds on it."

We shook hands on the wager. That day surely marked the beginning of a change for Hammer, and although Tony had sold out for what might have been a very reasonable sum, he told me later that he had miscalculated something.

Journey to the Unknown had been an exciting and challenging assignment and it taught me a lot, in addition to taking me another rung up the ladder. Joan Harrison even suggested that I should go to America and join her there as an associate producer. I wonder why I never did (although we came close to working together again when she and Eric made their home in Europe). Something else was a tremendous thrill on the series: I got my first screen credit. Then such things were hard-earned, as one had to be engaged in a semi-senior position to warrant the privilege. Nowadays everyone gets a credit, resulting in the end roller title racing through so fast you can't read any of the names, or it runs for so long that the composer has to write an entire symphony to keep everything going. Making titles costs money, so maybe lower-budget films could sell credits to anyone who would be prepared to work for 10 percent less than their normal rate. Just a thought.

The penultimate title reward is the so-called single card; the ultimate is when your name goes on the poster. For me a lot of water was yet to flow under the bridge before then.

· 8 ·

Brainless

The only copy in existence of the *Frankenstein Must Be Destroyed* script was on the top deck of a London bus. It was unaccompanied.

Bert Batt, who had just completed his first draft, had gone to visit Tony Keys at his home in Twickenham in West London. Being a non-driver, he had had to go by public transport to the appointed stop. Within seconds he realized what he'd left on a seat, but already the bus was making good its getaway. Hurrying to Tony's nearby house, he blurted out the bad news. Into ANK's car they piled, and the chase was on. Wonderful suspense. Each corner they rounded, they prayed the bus would come into sight. If only they could overtake it, Bert could leap from the car and re-board at the next stop. . . . Apparently, the hard work of four months was eventually retrieved at the bus depot at the end of the run.

Shooting was scheduled for spring 1969, and, with great loyalty, ANK invited me to join him on the film as production manager. Later I was secretly to discover that I was not his first choice, but that was to be expected; I'd not yet graduated to that somewhat elevated status. It was hardly surprising, therefore, that the usual production secretary on his films refused to work as my assistant, no doubt in the belief that at the tender age of twenty-six I was beneath her in experience—true enough. (I wonder what she would think about the young studio executives of today.) But to be fair to the lady in question, she did come up to me a few years later when I had become a producer and most kindly complimented me on how I was doing. In the meantime I was given someone else, who was quite famous for doing "The Gestetner Rock"—as call sheets were run off, she would dance energetically to the clackety rhythm of the duplicating machine.

Things didn't go very well from my end, and at one point during the pre-production period, ANK said in exasperation, "I'll make a production manager of you even if it kills me."

He remained his warm self, but at the time I figured he got on my back rather a lot.

As well as being the writer (and a pretty good one), Bert was the first assistant director, and with him was our old third assistant, who had been promoted to my past job as second assistant. I was really rather envious of him and felt very much alone and out of it. This was rubbed home when I went down to the stage halfway through our first day of principal photography. The sets were the instantly revampable ones Bernie Robinson was famous for—inside out and round about, so as to get the maximum use out of the studio floor space. I could hear the unit somewhere in the middle of a maze of flats and see the spill from the lights spreading up to the roof, but I couldn't find any way in. Eventually I arrived ignominiously at the side of the camera via an open fireplace.

The worst part of being a production manager is that if anything goes wrong, it is unquestionably his or her fault, and if it goes right, no credit is ever given. My five years in the job were certainly not my happiest, and I wasn't really cut out for the job.

With that off my chest, I can say that there were quite a lot of pleasures on this *Frankenstein*, not least being the presence of Peter Cushing—immaculate and precise as ever. Playing his assistant was a young actor called Simon Ward. Right from the start, it was apparent that Simon would go far. And in the director's chair was dear Terry Fisher. Although reasonably recovered from his accident at the end of *The Devil Rides Out*, he had become reliant on a walking stick and he looked older and frailer, but his mirth was unimpaired.

Freddie Jones was, at the age of forty, a comparative newcomer to acting in films—until then, I believe, he had been a schoolmaster. As Frankenstein's latest creation, he gave a remarkably sympathetic performance—a bit dotty, but it worked. He was at the start of a prolific career.

Veronica Carlson acquitted herself well enough as the girl, Anna Spengler. She also managed to escape the nudity that was about to become *de rigeur* for later Hammer productions and most others, actually, as the censorship guidelines relaxed. My frank opinion is that nudity demeaned the work. Of course, the argument for it was to give a boost in audience numbers in an ailing industry. Or was it to give a boost to ageing film salesmen? Don't get me wrong here, I have nothing against nudity on screen when it occurs as a natural part of the narrative, and I have been responsible for writing scenes with high sexual content. But, I mean to say! Topless bisexual vampires! Even in his wildest dreams Bram Stoker wouldn't have envisioned such a thing—at least I don't think so.

There are written reports that during a scene where Frankenstein rapes Anna, the actress became distressed and the thoughtful Peter Cushing called a halt to the proceedings. I have to say I cannot recall the incident. That's not to say it didn't happen, and if it did, it just goes to prove the remoteness of a production manager.

Also in the cast was an actor called Frank Middlemass. During my schoolboy days he was in repertory theatre in Canterbury and, because of my fascination with the stage, he had kindly taken a friend and me under his wing. It was therefore rather extraordinary that even though he knew perfectly well who I was, he barely acknowledged me on this production. Perhaps this was yet another indication of the hapless world of management.

Sprightly Yorkshireman, Harold Godwin, with whom I had worked during my time at Beaconsfield, took on the role of a burglar. He gets caught and loses his head for his troubles, and the head gets kicked across a room. So convincing was his portrayal and so convincing was the mock-up head that he had to leave the screening room during rushes the next day. Shortly afterward I discovered him wandering up and down a corridor and moaning with his hands on either side of his head to ensure it was still there. I comforted him as best I could. The whole episode was extraordinary, but gives a wonderful example of how Hammer's gothic horror movies affected more than just the audience.

The most gruesome sequence in the movie is where Frankenstein, pushing his experiments to the limit, performs a brain transplant. This was when I ran into a bit of further trouble with ANK. No brain was there when the crew were ready to film this delicate task. Was it really down to me? Surely Bernard Robinson, as the designer, should have made sure this essential prop was to hand? If not him, then why not the property master? And why hadn't the second assistant checked up on it as we had been taught?

"At the end of the day, it's your responsibility," Tony Keys told me with a degree of grimness, as the unit stood around unable to shoot.

I rushed round to the art department. No Bernie, and his assistants were not able to help. "Oh God!" Time is money. Then someone came up with an idea. Get some brains from a butcher's shop. The largest available were sheep brains—not nearly big enough. So I bought three and rushed them back to the prop man and asked him to somehow stick them together. He did his best with a needle and thread, but when the whole (looking quite good) was submerged into a glass tank of some sort of bubbling solution, the three segments separated and then started to disintegrate. Hopeless. While hurrying back to the art department to get them to do something to help, I saw Bernie drive through the studio entrance.

"Bernie," I panted out, "where have you been?"

Apparently he had started his day by checking out how the dressing was going on a location.

"We haven't got a brain!"

"Well of course we have a brain," he responded phlegmatically.

A few minutes later we were in his office, and he took the perfect mock-up specimen from a cupboard. I rushed it to the set, still wondering why none of his staff knew of its existence.

An hour of the shooting day lost and Tony Keys alarmed at my inefficiency! Then something else went wrong, and for once it could not be laid at my door. The special effects device that caused the solution in the brain tank to bubble stopped working. Various people from Les Bowie's team spent another forty-five minutes trying to fix the problem. They didn't succeed, but by then Les, himself, had arrived after receiving an emergency call. His remedy, on considering the problem from a first-hand perspective, was the simplest known to man. He dropped in four Alka-Seltzer tablets and we were up and running once more.

A relieved Tony Keys bought me an undeserved lunch that day.

During the shooting period there was an evening event that I was most eager to attend: the Royal Command Performance of a wonderful film directed by my father—*The Prime of Miss Jean Brodie*. It was to be on a Wednesday when the *Frankenstein* crew were scheduled to be shooting late on the lot. I asked Tony Keys if I might be allowed to go, but he very firmly told me my duty was to stay with the production I was supposed to be managing. I was disappointed and said as much to Ronnie, who wholeheartedly agreed with Tony. I did make it to the dinner after the performance, though. This is an example of Tony carrying out his statement that he would make something of me even in the face of his own demise. Yes, he gave me some hard times, but they set me a standard of which I am now proud. Would that similar standards existed today.

A week later I was using the Les Bowie Alka-Seltzer remedy on myself. It just hit me overnight—a fever of 103 and a bit, a splitting headache, and a world going in and out of focus. A severe case of flu was the diagnosis, and I had to remain bedridden for a week. Apart from half a day off with a similar complaint in the late 1970s, I am happy to be able to report I haven't otherwise been absent from work—yet. Standards again, I suppose.

The film completed shooting during that rotten week, with no one the worse for wear by my absence, and on the Saturday I received a letter from Peter Cushing. His delicate hand expressed his gratitude for what I had done (can't think of anything in particular) and his wishes for my speedy recovery. So very thoughtful and kind of him. It was signed Peter and Helen. Even after her untimely death, he always ended with both their names. But that terrible moment in his life still lay before him.

The next week I was back at my lonely desk for the postproduction work. Although this is invariably a less hectic time than the actual shooting period, it is, as a result, rather boring—mainly a task of tidying things up, merged with title-making, looping, et cetera. Then on one bright day we had a nice surprise; Tony Hinds dropped in at the studio for lunch. He said how much he had been enjoying his retirement over the last ten or so months and still had no intention of returning to the industry. Accepting my probable defeat over our wager, I wrote him a check for ten pounds. If only I had made the bet that he'd be back at work within two years rather than one, the ten pounds would have been mine. In any event, sadly, his career as a producer was over, and when he did start again it was as a writer. Some time later I asked him why he'd changed his mind.

"For the money. I didn't reckon on inflation growing so rapidly." The punitive interest rates as well.

Meanwhile the second bolt of lightning caught Terry Fisher off guard and under much the same circumstances as it had before—a few too many drinks and crossing a road without looking. Knocked down again!

Frankenstein Must Be Destroyed was the last film I was to do with Tony Keys, and it was the penultimate one he was to make. We remained in touch as he tried to get various projects off the ground, and I did several budgets and schedules for him—by then he obviously must have had faith in me. But time was running out; he was now nearing sixty. In 1972 he coproduced, with Christopher Lee, a thriller movie for the Rank Organization. He asked me to work on it, but very unfortunately I was on another production.

Tony had been a wonderful teacher, and his knowledge of the nuts and bolts of the industry was enormous. If he had a failing as a producer it was because of this very fact. By that I mean his focus was on day-to-day affairs rather than creative matters, and that can be a problem when the age thing catches up with a person. Had he been a writer, he could have gone on for years. During the mid-seventies his health let him down. He recovered from his heart attack, but the vim had gone out of him. Then his wife, Maggie, became ill and Tony had to nurse her back to full strength, which he did in the fullness of time. When we had lunch together in 1984 at his golf club in Richmond, he was enthusiastic on my behalf, as I was to produce a film from a Graham Greene novel starring Alec Guinness. He told me how he would like to get back to producing and how much he missed the life. Anthony Nelson Keys died in early 1985. God bless him.

Anthony Hinds's longtime secretary, Pam Anderson, had recently left the company, no doubt because of the departure of her boss, and joined Tigon Films as an assistant to the managing director, Tony Tenser. During the sixties and early seventies Tenser's output had been Hammer-type productions, largely of a lower quality and at even lower cost, and sexploitation movies. Pam, a middle-aged woman whose outward severity masked a warm friendliness beneath, suggested I should join them as their production manager. As a married man with two children, having a job was essential—I'd have even been happy to go back to being a second assistant director, a job I had been out of for little more than a year—so I leapt at the chance of joining Tigon. Actually it was a deep-end assignment, as I found myself to be head of production—a grand title, but there was no one else around to be head of. Shared secretarial assistance was about as far as it went.

Rapidly I had to learn how to do budgets and see to all the pre-production work from the outset and take a film all the way through to delivery to the in-house distributors. It is astonishing that someone of my limited experience was given so much autonomy. The first film I was to tackle had Dennis Waterman in place for the lead, but the script was dire and my tenderfoot screenwriting skills were certainly not up to improving it. So I canceled the production and, believe it or not, no one batted an eyelid—except the director, who was more than a bit upset!

As other productions went through the mill, I found myself in the cutting rooms more and more and getting myself involved in the complex world of sales as well. During my time there, we made a couple of goodish pictures. *Monique* has to fall into the sex-film category, but it rose above the norm by having a well-written script, which dealt with a ménage à trois in a sensitive and understated way and was further enhanced with a score by the brilliant French jazz musician, Jacques Loussier. Old chum Moray Grant was the cinematographer; his work with Tigon would lead him back to Hammer in this capacity. The producer was Michael Style, who was totally inexperienced in film production, having run an operation supplying video equipment and stage space. (A pleasant enough person, who was, I gather, the friend of a friend of someone.) Coincidentally, his setup had been the one responsible for the only episode of *Journey to the Unknown* to have been farmed out.

Shortly Michael came up with the idea of developing a script, from a story by the nineteenth-century Irish novelist J. Sheridan Le Fanu. This was eventually to be called *The Vampire Lovers*. I cannot think why it was not snapped up by Tigon, but it wasn't, and Hammer did it instead.

Moray joined Michael, and I was sorely tempted to take up the offer to go with them, but I couldn't leave my current employers without serving them with a correct period of notice or, at the very least, having a damn good reason to jump ship. Perhaps the reason existed. . . .

At around this time Tony Tenser was intent on cashing in on the blooming sex market and productions of that kind were not for me. I begged him to junk one, half completed, rubbishy film of this genre, but he rightly argued that by doing so he would be throwing away a lot of money. I was instructed to see it finished because, if there was a beginning, middle, and end, he'd be able to sell it to someone sooner or later—and eventually he did. But Tony and I were moving in different directions. My aim was to see more creative work coming from our endeavours, so how could I swallow his passing up a script that was, in my opinion, just right for us? After all, he had produced a couple of excellent and successful movies with Roman Polanski—*Repulsion* and *Cul-de-sac*.

No—he favoured making a version of *Fanny Hill* on a shoestring budget. (Given enough money to make it elegantly, I would have been happy to go along with the idea.) Over many days I pitched and repitched to him the script of *Young Man, I Think You're Dying* in an attempt to persuade him to finance that film. But without success.

In the middle of the following week he flew off to New York for sales meetings, and that's when I received a call from Roy Skeggs at Hammer—now raised to the post of "in charge of production." "For the last time, do you want to do *Vampire Lovers*?"

"Will you give me till Monday? You know I want to come with you, but first I have to sort everything out here."

Tenser's financier and business partner, Laurie Marsh, was in our offices that Friday morning, and I told him of the situation and how much I was tempted to return to the old company, because no interesting future was appearing on the current horizon.

"Look," he said, "I know you and Tony have been having your differences of opinion, but it has to be dealt with. Get yourself out to New York this afternoon and tidy up the mess once and for all."

"This afternoon!"

"This afternoon."

No passport! And anyway my U.S. visa had expired.

"Then you can use your production managerial skills to sort it out," he said, semi-helpfully.

I called my old friend, the one who had rescued me when my car broke down during *Journey to the Unknown*.

"Help!" I bleated.

Then I made a call to Heather to tell her what was happening and that she should give our friend my passport and would she please pack a small bag for me. My friend kindly shot up to London and met me at the American Embassy. An hour later I was in possession of all the required stamps of approval and an hour afterwards at Heathrow airport collecting a waiting ticket for the five o'clock Pan Am flight.

Tony met me at Kennedy, and we continued our usual arguments for or against our various choices of product. I can only imagine that Laurie had told him about my imminent desertion, because by the time we reached Manhattan, Tony had agreed to go with *Young Man*. What I have never understood is why anyone in his position would ever have listened to me. With the roles reversed, I'd have told someone who was essentially a parvenu to get lost.

"And now you're here," said Tony as we pulled up at the hotel, "you might as well learn a bit about the practical side of film sales."

It was a wonderful and very educational few days.

I phoned Roy Skeggs from New York to say I couldn't get back to Hammer, and, in due course, we went into preproduction with our film. Beryl Reid, of recent *The Killing of Sister George* fame, was the star, along with Dame Flora Robson. This revered actress, who always looked old before her time, was really rather too grand to play in our low-budget piece. She subsequently told me she had been of a mind to decline our paltry offer when she met Laurence Olivier on the train back to their close-by homes in Brighton. His advice to her was to take any job in these difficult times that would help pay the rent! She did.

The end result was pretty good, although disappointingly Tony changed the title to *The Beast in the Cellar*. And we were back to arguing again. This time it was over the music. Hemdale had become Tigon's new partners and for a brief period I became a director of the former company. It was all very political and, had it not been for David Hemmings, untenable. He and I would sit in the boardroom at opposite sides of the table and grin at each other or nudge feet as one ludicrous idea after another was put forward at each of our weekly meetings.

Anyway, Hemdale had a famous composer (who had a gorgeous blonde chauffeuse), and he was assigned to our film, just like that. The director, James Kelly, the producer, Graham Harris, and I all believed the music to be utterly wrong.

Tony came to Pinewood Studios where we were in postproduction and was adamant that the score had to be used.

I then came out with one of the most arrogant remarks of all time.

"Well, if you insist on this composer, you can shove my contract up your arse."

I was still fuming with creative anger when an hour later the telephone rang. It was Tony's lawyer.

"Mr. Tenser has decided to take your suggestion. You're out." Happily he added, "With a month's pay."

Life is odd. By prior arrangement Heather and I were to have had lunch with Tony and his wife at his home in Kent the next weekend, and we kept the appointment. A lovely day was had by all of us, with no hard feelings. And we had another child to display. Darling little Emma Neame was just a month old.

Tony and I have always kept in touch, and at one point we even formed a company together called Team (a mixture of Tenser and Neame); to this day, we exchange Christmas cards. Perhaps he was a lesser showman than Jimmy Carreras, but most certainly he had *chutzpah*.

The other odd thing was that I stayed on at Pinewood to complete the film, even though no longer a part of Tigon. And Tony's music stayed! We even sat together at the preview. . . .

Shortly I became "available" (i.e., out of work) and could only hope something might come my way—preferably another assignment with Hammer. It did, and I instantly became excited, because nearly eighteen months of absence from the people who had become firm friends was too long.

Little did anyone suspect that during the filming of *Blood from the Mummy's Tomb*, two deaths would occur and that both would mean a lot to everyone, however far removed from direct involvement.

· 9 ·

Razor Blades and a Hand

"*B*ad news," Roy Skeggs announced through the internal phone at EMI (formerly ABPC) Studios.

Roy, whom I had first met properly on *Journey to the Unknown*, is a broad, oval-faced fellow with a chuckling sense of humor that belies his more serious background as an accountant. Sometimes he still wears an accountant's style of tie. For many years he had been based at the grandly named Hammer House in Wardour Street—the only street in London considered to be shady on both sides!—but he had not long since been appointed to a grander position and was now based at Elstree.

"Seth Holt has failed his medical examination," he continued.

Medical insurance is considered an essential part of the overall protection of a production. If a director becomes ill or dies during the shooting schedule, time could be lost and the cost of it is recoverable from the underwriters. Insurance against losing the services of actors in the days before computer-generated imaging (such as was used to replace Oliver Reed in *Gladiator*) was similarly critical. But such a policy for directors, unless they were at the very top of the tree, always seemed a bit pointless to me because they could, theoretically, be replaced at a moment's notice. And Seth was to be the director of *Blood from the Mummy's Tomb*.

"Better carry on as we are without the cover, don't you think?" said Roy.

"Yes, I agree." My response was given lightly because, in a way, he'd already made the decision for us.

Seth Holt didn't help himself. He had already had a heart attack because of obesity brought on by a more than healthy appetite, alcohol, and way, way too many cigarettes. It's true that by now he'd lost weight, but the drinking and smoking continued, and his much younger wife, Sally, did little to discourage him. Seth had been one of England's best film editors and was responsible for his end of the storytelling on many Ealing comedies. He also edited the wonderful *Saturday Night and Sunday Morning*. As a director, his work was limited, although he had an instinctive talent (one of his pictures had been the other Hammer film with Bette Davis—*The Nanny*).

He brought along with him his own editor. Oswald Haffenrichter was highly regarded in the industry; his credits include *The Third Man* and *The Fallen Idol*, both for Carol Reed.

The producer of our production was an engaging American publicity man named Howard Brandy. Hammer's policy was to appoint whoever came up with the idea for a film as its producer. Usually they were without any experience, and our job (Roy Skeggs's and, in this case, mine) was to make them feel comfortable and then just get on with the film regardless of their producing talents or lack of them. This sounds ridiculously self-seeking, but it really was so. Howard was a pleasant enough person out of place, but he had brought the company a version of Bram Stoker's *Jewell of the 7 Stars*, which fitted the bill.

Peter Cushing was to star in the role of Professor Fuchs, an Egyptologist, and several other very interesting actors were cast, including George Couloris, Rosalie Crutchley, and the irrepressible James Villiers—he of good wit. Valerie Leon (an ex-model) was set for the female lead. More of her and her anatomy anon.

The first hurdle to be overcome was a national one-day strike threat by two unions: NATKE, which represented the studio craftsmen, and the ETU, for the electricians and (for the life of me I can't think why) plumbers. This, if it happened, was to occur on the Tuesday of our first week of shooting. Bryan Forbes, who at the time had been appointed head of the studio (another mystery) called me to his office and advised me to postpone production by a week. It was not a good suggestion, as a week's delay would cost more than a lost day.

"So what'll you do?" asked Bryan.

"If your studio staff don't turn up for work, you can't charge us for their services and then I'll call *force majeure* on the freelance crew we are employing directly." Not that I thought I'd ever get away with it, but there was another card I had up my sleeve. A set had been prepared and pre-lit, so shooting might just be able to continue without the studio crew. In a kind of way it was a weather cover, although nothing whatsoever to do with inclemency; call it a union protection plan.

Bryan wished me luck and washed his hands of the affair.

The proposed strike was called off on the Thursday before filming commenced, but even so, something made the little bell in my head ring and warned me not to cancel the alternative day's work on our readied set, regardless of the extra cost of stage rental.

The first day of filming was fine, with Peter Cushing released early by prearrangement so he could go back to his home in Whitstable to be with his chronically ill wife, Helen. This was a pattern we planned to follow whenever possible. In the evening the second assistant director telephoned him to give him his on-set call time for Tuesday. Peter was in tears. Helen had taken a drastic turn for the worse and was not expected to live through the night. There and then our leading player had to resign from the film.

It was terribly heartrending, as the couple had remained very much in love. Helen died as predicted. Once he had overcome his initial grief Peter immersed himself in work on many subsequent productions, but there was always a side of him that desperately wanted to be reunited with her. As a devout man he could not take his own life, but he had always been another fairly heavy smoker and now increased his intake, seemingly happy for it to stop him in his tracks. Still the professional actor, Peter started to wear white cotton gloves, similar to the ones used by film editors, so as to avoid nicotine stains on his fingers, which would be out of character for a baron or other roles he played.

Naturally, as is always the case, the show had to go on, and arrangements were made for Andrew Keir to step into the part. What with costuming, the insurance medical exam, and time for him to study the script, it was remarkable that he would be able to start work on Wednesday. What to do on the Tuesday? Well, luckily the set prepared for shooting in the event of the strike was for scenes not featuring Professor Fuchs. So the schedule was met for the second day. This stroke of good fortune came about because of the bell in my head. I learned something else from that sad occasion; even though one should not cross bridges until one comes to them, it is pretty helpful to know where they lie should they be needed. It has paid off on more than a few occasions.

From this time on, Sally Hyman, my usually ebullient secretary, was convinced that the production was cursed. Her claim was that the mock-up Ancient Egyptian artifacts created by art director Scott Macgregor gave off bad karma. After the brain incident on the last *Frankenstein*, I had wanted to keep these essential props in my shared office. But she would have none of it. In the end we reached a compromise and the most offensive, in her eyes, were stored elsewhere. Nevertheless, perhaps Sally was right; some unpleasant events were to come about, one of them very personal to me.

There were, however, lighter moments. An actor named Aubrey Morris had the part of an unfortunate man who has his throat torn out by the Valerie Leon character in the guise of the reborn and avenging mummy. He arrived on set with a prosthetic patch covering his Adam's apple from which protruded his glistening jugular vein and more. We sent him across the road to Borehamwood's pharmacy to ask innocently if they could sell him a packet of safety razor blades for use in the future. And then there was the incident of the severed mummy's hand, which sort of walked about on its own. The effect was created by having someone beneath a rostrum with a long slot cut out of it and desert sand piled on top—a sliding piece of hardboard stopped too much of the sand from dropping through the slot as the hand moved—and more prosthetic dangles were attached to the back of its owner's angled wrist. The severed hand was also present in other scenes. Before it was used for the first time, I recall taking it down to the set for approval by Seth and being seen entering the stage by various members of the crew.
"Another poor sod's been caught fiddling his expenses," Roddy Barron, the clapper boy, quite wittily remarked.
The next few weeks of filming continued well, and Sally's premonition seemed groundless. That was until the end of the penultimate week.

Roy Skeggs and I were getting on well together, and the unit began to see us as a bit of a double act. (This is borne out by a prop estate agent's sign outside a house on one of our locations: "Skeggs & Neame"—mind you, if I had known about it beforehand, it would not have been allowed in the film.) The next production Hammer was to make was a feature from the successful TV series *On the Buses,* and Roy wanted me to be the production manager while he watched over the inexperienced incoming producers (the writers of the series). I was all set to start work on the schedule at home on the Sunday when the first of two ghastly things happened. Heather and I got into a rotten argument, which, although triggered by some ultimately trivial matter, was actually a continuation of differences that had been ongoing for eighteen months or more. For me, enough was enough, and for her, too. By ten o'clock in the morning we had finally accepted that there was no alternative but to seek a divorce. As I write these words I am ashamed at how unfeeling they must sound, but we were both adamant and I had work to do. This was all part of furthering my career and not putting my family first, as should have been the case. I was as guilty as anyone can be of paying more attention to a low-budget comedy picture than to the future of my own beloved children.

Then the telephone rang. It was Seth Holt's wife. She got straight to the point. "Seth has died."

"What!"

"We had some friends over for dinner last night and at the end of the meal he looked at me and said, 'I'm going, Sal.'" Apparently he had toppled sideways and was dead by the time he reached the floor. Too much alcohol and too many cigarettes had got to him by his forty-ninth year. We should have seen it coming. For the whole of the previous week he had been suffering from hiccups. On Tuesday we had called in a doctor, who did not diagnose anything too serious; the same happened again on Thursday, although this time he was given some medication. On Friday, we were to shoot a sandstorm on the stage with masses of fuller's earth being blown around. The scene was ready to be filmed at about 10:00 A.M. The third assistant director was dispatched to call Seth from the dressing room we had specially arranged for him to relax in when not required on the stage. He was sitting in a chair with his eyes closed and made no response to the third's call. The young man came into my office, his face ashen. He concluded his report by saying, "I think he may be dead."

I hurried along to the dressing room, knocked at the door and entered without waiting for a reply. "Seth!"

The poor man hiccupped and slowly his eyes opened. "Yes?"
"We're ready for a rehearsal."
Slowly he got to his feet and I accompanied him to the set. "You should leave the stage for the actual shooting because of all the dust flying about."
"Oh, no. I'll stay by the camera," he protested.
In addition to his other medical problems, Seth had asthma, and I knew it would be very foolish indeed for him to remain there in such circumstances.
"Please don't. Wait outside the door and I'll call you as soon as it's over and give you a full report."
But he was determined to carry out his duties. For certain the dust was a contributory factor in what happened on Saturday.
By lunchtime the scene was in the can and Seth seemed to be all right—apart from those wretched hiccups that continued through the takes. Concerned they were putting too much strain on his heart, we called in the doctor yet again. And yet again he played down the problem.
The work scheduled for the afternoon was more congenial, and Seth was able to sit beside the camera in a relaxed way. He smoked and had his glass of whisky in his hand . . . and he hiccupped.

Then came the fateful phone call at ten o'clock on Sunday morning. I spent a short while commiserating with his wife and rather uselessly asked if there was anything I could do, or anything she needed.
As soon as I told him, Roy got in touch with our executive producer, Michael Carreras (once again back with Hammer), and we all agreed to meet at the studio after lunch. There, I made calls to the entire crew and cast and broke the bad news. Some took it more sanguinely than others; our continuity girl burst into tears.
In an obituary published in one of the U.K.'s more upmarket newspapers, the writer expressed his regret that Seth Holt had not lived long enough to make his definitive film; simply, it had been around the corner he was not destined to turn.

The plan was for Michael to take over directing, starting the following morning, and I would arrange for him to see the rushes of Friday's work as soon as possible. The editors arrived especially early and by

8:15 A.M. we were in the screening room. It was desperately sad; throughout every shot we could hear the late Seth's hiccups.

Half an hour later Michael was on the stage and preparing his first setup. In hindsight it seems all far too clinical; after all, we had lost just fifteen minutes from our schedule as a result of the tragedy. It just goes to show we had no need for insurance cover on our director.

The set was subdued, but then the tension was broken by a mildly amusing remark made by Neil Binney, the camera operator. Over-the-top hoots of laughter from everyone and we were callously back on course.

The funeral was held four days later with a Victorian hearse drawn by four black horses bearing the coffin to the church in true Hammer style. Several people on the crew wanted to attend the service, but after much deliberation it was decided that Seth would have preferred us to carry on with his last film. Roy went to represent us all.

During that last week, I had some second-unit directing to do. I seemed to be specializing in this field, although always uncredited—just as well, on this particular occasion. It was a car crash sequence, but we didn't have the funds to do it as it really should have been done. I discussed an idea with Michael, which he fully supported and, in fact, decided to employ in a couple of similar scenes he was to shoot. The crash would be made up of a series of rapidly cut together frozen frame shots, their colour drained and manipulated in a disturbing way. These would be filmed with a movie camera so as to maintain a similar quality to the main unit's work and then turned into still images by selecting the best frame in each setup. To achieve this I got the actors and extras into a nearly fixed position and then ran the camera for about thirty seconds while they made small adjustments to their positions and expressions to give us a good selection to choose from—over seven hundred still picture options per angle! In principle the plan was sound, but I was horrified when I eventually got to see the completed film at a special screening at London's National Film Theatre—the editor had simply put the shots together without freezing them or draining the colour. (Had I been aware of this at the time, I would certainly have created a fuss, but by then I was busy with *On the Buses*. The end result looked utterly ridiculous. Why had Michael let this happen?) Recently I read rather a good review of the movie, which only turned a bit sour when it came to this scene: "Terribly, terribly done." I concur.

Another bit I was responsible for was nearly as bad. It was a short sequence with Valerie Leon. For some reason she had to run through a thick wood wearing a negligée over a seriously push-up bra. We could not afford the transport to go on location, so somewhere had to be found on the lot. This wasn't easy, as suburban houses were on three of its boundaries and the studio buildings on the fourth. There was, however, a short, single line of spindly poplar trees. Thanks to my camera department days I could find a way of making it work. By positioning the camera at the end of the line and slightly to one side and by utilizing a very long focus lens, it actually appeared as if we were in a wood. The camera was run at ninety-six frames per second (for a slow-motion dramatic effect) and the girl came toward us. Valerie's bosom was awesome, but as she ran each breast was out of synchronization with the other and the effect was exacerbated by the slow motion. My cinematic magic had succeeded in making an attractive young woman look far from her best!

It is customary to have a wrap party at the end of shooting. However, in view of what had so recently happened, we thought such a celebration would be in poor taste. Instead, the money it would have cost was given to Sally Holt to help her through the next few difficult weeks. Having said that, all the crew, actors, and management staff congregated in the studio bar, bought each other drinks, toasted Seth's memory, and sighed with relief that this trying production was behind them.

I had only two weeks to wrap up my production manager's work and prepare for the next film, while at the same time moving out of my family home.

Early the next Saturday morning, I went into the bedroom they shared to say goodbye to my son and eldest daughter. They didn't understand what was happening and I couldn't have explained to them—I simply said I would see them again soon. Baby Emma was in a crib in another room. At barely six months old, this tiny being was the one who could never ever understand. Yet, with tears welling in my eyes, I tried to tell her I was not leaving her and I would always be there for her and for Gareth and for Shuna.

It is good to be able to add that we did remain close, and we still are.

Difficult times, but, to use one of my father's favorite expressions—"Crash on, regardless."

Both Michael Carreras and his wife, Jo, were very kind and thoughtful even to the point of inviting me to their Gloucestershire home for a weekend. "Michael makes a sensational curry," Jo informed me.

He was really full of life at this time, because, having recently returned from his freelance period, he had now taken over from his father as owner and head of Hammer. But, as touched upon earlier, I was shortly to witness him baring his teeth.

Old Ossie Haffenrichter, Seth's *schnittmeister*, was not a neat worker by any standards, and there were various stories about him circulating around that, whether apocryphal or not, were an indication of it. Most editors wear cotton gloves while handling film, and when they make an actual cut in the celluloid they do so with precision equipment. Not Ossie. He would figure out how many seconds a particular shot should remain on the screen and then, like a haberdasher, measure out a length of film and tear it off jaggedly with his teeth. He had also been known to go home with small rolls of rushes stuffed in his baggy jacket pockets. Ossie was another heavy smoker, and the most famous story of all was about when he accidentally dropped a cigarette end into a bin of nitrate film. He was lucky not to have killed himself and burned the studio down in the bargain. True or not, there is rarely smoke without fire!

We were in the projection room looking at a sequence when Michael suddenly exploded. His complaint was certainly justified. The footage was all terribly scratched and patched up. "How can you do this to my film?" he roared at Ossie, who smiled sheepishly in response. Half an hour later, he and his assistant were summarily fired. A little uncalled for, I thought. Such a thing can break a strong man's heart.

On the Buses, which starred Reg Varney, was a memorable product from the company. It was all right as a piece of light work, but its claim to fame was that we produced it for under one hundred thousand pounds and that within weeks of its release it became Hammer's quickest domestic earner. This was one of the earliest examples of a TV series becoming a feature film, and what a clever idea it was. The audience was already there, and for most of the fans, it would be the first time they could see the stars in color. The director was a small bearded man called Harry Booth. He was pleasant enough, albeit a bit uninspired, but it didn't matter; all he had to do was photograph the already created characters doing what was written in the script. And he made a good enough job of that.

I will not dwell on the film here, as it is not the kind of movie to attract Hammer aficionados in general terms. Suffice it to say, the filming went like clockwork, and I finished the tidying up process ahead of time. I recall feeling rather proud that I was still on the payroll while wallowing in a California swimming pool. My father and mother were there as Ronnie prepared to direct *The Poseidon Adventure,* and I joined them for a month.

By midsummer, and after a most relaxing break, I was back at Elstree doing my own preparation for what I thought was going to be one of the best pictures I would be involved with for Hammer.

· 10 ·

Bludlust

𝓑olney is a pretty village set in the midst of England's rolling South Downs and not far from the Sussex seaside resort of Brighton. During the second half of the nineteenth century, an eccentric Bavarian gentleman built a massive *schloss* there. Passing through the ornate gates, one immediately expects to hear the sound of oompah bands and see maidens serving great foaming steins of beer to men in lederhosen straddled about beneath the slate-grey turrets. On my first visit, a vivid blue sky rose like a dome above them, adding to the crisp Middle European atmosphere. Quite why the place was there at all was unknown, but then the entrepreneur behind it was, as I said, eccentric. The property had recently been lovingly restored to its former glory, and the owners seemed eager enough to recoup some of their investment by allowing us to film there in return for a location fee.

The script of *Blood Will Have Blood* was by Christopher Wicking, who had also written *Blood from the Mummy's Tomb*. In my opinion he is an erratic writer, but this one was good. It moved laterally to look at the gothic horror world in a way different from the expected one, with much visual imagery used to tell the story. Yes, it's fair to say that some of the dialogue is a bit heavy-handed, but that is probably because of an imbalance between what is heard and what is seen. The story was by Frank Godwin, a mild-mannered man who came across as a bit of a holiday resort organizer type—I mean no disrespect, simply that one could imagine he had an apple in his pocket, a piece of chalk, and a whistle. He was also to be the producer. In such a capacity, Frank had made some good films, most notably early kitchen-sink dramas with director J. Lee Thompson like *Woman in a Dressing Gown* and *No Trees in the Street*. It must have been very difficult for him with Roy Skeggs and me, because the two of us had formed a good way of working together. Each of us knew exactly what the other was taking responsibility for—and, being used to simply titular producers, we unquestionably gave him little say in the actual operation of production.

This was wrong, particularly in light of Frank's own experience and the fact that he had cleverly pitched the idea to the Hammer executives by intriguing them with an obscure word he claimed to have discovered in some old manuscripts: *Bludlust*. It looked vaguely German, but in fact it wasn't; it was absolute nonsense, and Frank had invented it. But what he did is a nice indication of how the simplest hook can draw finance into a project. Perhaps I should put that in the past tense . . . though maybe not!

The screenplay attracted an extremely good cast, including Robert (Tim) Hardy, an avid horseman who, a short while later, nearly lost his life in a riding accident, and Michael Hordern (later Sir Michael), Patrick Magee, Paul Jones (probably better known as a singer), and the always watchable Yvonne Mitchell, as well as newcomer Shane Briant. Marianne Faithfull was to have played the part of his sister but unfortunately had to drop out before filming commenced. Gillian Hills was engaged instead—a pretty girl who gave a convincing performance but, because she did not fit into the Hammer mold of the starlet, failed to attract the wider recognition she fairly deserved. This lack of recognition must also be said of Shane; although he has had some success in both his acting career and as a writer, I venture to say it has not been enough.

The familiar ring of the internal telephone:

"Christopher . . . er . . . well . . . er, it's Michael Stringer here . . ." Michael was our production designer. It would have been hard to find anyone better for the film, because he had a real sense of period dressing. Always light-handed and subtle in his style, he was also a bit uncertain when it came to practical matters like driving a car at over thirty miles an hour or picking up a telephone. We teased him about it:

"Well, hello, Michael Stringer, there," I replied to his introduction. A kind of flapping sound came down the line, if that makes any kind of sense.

"Er . . . Yes. . . ." And the line clicked off.

Thirty seconds later the phone rang again.

"Hello, Michael," I said. . . .

"How did you know it was me? That was very clever of you." And he really did mean it.

Cutting to the point, I inquired, "What can we do for you?"

"It's about the transport of furniture for the location interiors at Bolney."

"Fine, what do you need?"

"A small van on Friday."

"A small van!" I said in delighted astonishment. "I've penciled in a large truck for Wednesday."

"No, no, we won't need anything as big as that."

"Surely, if you're going to dress the main hall the way it would have looked in the nineteenth century, you'll need a stack of furniture?"

It was a big hall.

"Do you think so?" he said with an edge of doubt in his voice.

"Don't you?"

"Not really, actually in those days there was very little furniture around, just the odd piece in the right place."

I went along with him, happy in the knowledge I was going to be able to make a transport budget saving.

He was, of course, quite right. A lesser designer would have attempted to show grandeur by quantity rather than subtlety. This one set established the overall style of the film and gave the whole a three-dimensional quality—ideally suited to the long-established family in the narrative.

When writing a book like this, the Internet Movie Data Base is a very useful tool for jogging thirty-year-old memories, but sometimes its accuracy needs questioning. I am credited there as being the production designer of what, for some reason best known to the salesmen, became *Demons of the Mind*. This reduces the invaluable contribution of Michael Stringer, but try and alter information on a website!

The compact and smiling Peter Sykes was the director and kept his finger on the pulse just about all the time. Only once did I witness a lack of clear direction. Michael Hordern's character was that of a dotty, wandering priest, who becomes even more befuddled when caught in the midst of pillaging villagers. Peter instructed him to rise shakily after being knocked to the ground and make his way off camera.

"Ready to shoot!" cried the assistant director. "Light the fires! Smoke pots! Roll 'em!"

"Sound speed!"

"Two-forty-seven, take one."

Clap from the clapper board.

"Background action!"

And the extras started charging around with cudgels as instructed.

"Action," called Peter to Michael.

Michael entered. Got pushed down. Rolled over and, with dazed expression, slowly got to his feet while the melee continued around him. Ever the professional when doubt set in, he turned his back to the camera....

"Peter! You didn't tell me which way to exit."

"To your left."

"Left?"

"Yes, left."

"Right."

Michael exited to the left. The shot, minus this confusing and amusing exchange on the soundtrack, is in the completed film.

I was to work with Peter Sykes again on *The Irish R.M.,* a 1980s television series starring Peter Bowles. He needed tracking down for this assignment. We had lost touch after *Demons of the Mind,* and he was no longer to be found at his tasteful North London home. It is said you can find anyone within three well-aimed phone calls, and contact was made within that boundary (in my experience it has rarely been otherwise). He currently held a post teaching film at a university, but could be released on a sabbatical. (Long may this situation remain in higher education, whereby tutors are allowed to keep their hands in in the commercial world.) He did an excellent job on the production and then disappeared again. A good director of more than one Hammer film seems to have chosen another path. I wonder why. Certainly it was said that Seth Holt did not live long enough to make his definitive film. Neither, it seems, will Peter, and more's the pity.

There was someone else working on *Demons of the Mind* who has never been given sufficient public praise: Rosemary Burrows.

Lines of demarcation were rife during the trade-union heyday. Back in 1965 on *Circus of Fear* (the non-Hammer film made at Bray Studios) an incident happened that illustrates the utter stupidity of the situation.

A very heavy arc light was being hoisted onto a stand; an electrician, up on some steps, was helping to hoist it with a cord while two others heaved from below. Suddenly the back of one these men gave way. He staggered under the weight. I happened to be close by and moved in to take the weight from him. Had someone not done so, this massive piece of equipment would have fallen and seriously injured him. Rebalanced, the light was secured without harm to anyone.

Two days later I received a summons to appear before the local Electrical Trade Union shop to face the charge of touching something that lay absolutely within their realm. What made it all so ridiculous was the action was brought by the man whose back had failed him. If found guilty I was liable to be "branched." (I never knew what this meant, but, to use another obscure expression, I guess it's being sent to Coventry, so that no self-respecting electrician would work on the same set as me for a specified time determined by the "court.") I didn't bother to attend the hearing and, in any event, nothing came of it.

This is an example of how the unions would at least attempt to protect the interests of their ticket-holding and dues-paying brethren. To make it even more complicated, they were closed shops. This meant you could not get a job unless you were a member of the union, and you couldn't become a member of the union if you didn't have a job! Principally there existed the Association of Cinematograph Technicians (ACT) representing the "officer class"; the ETU, with the abovementioned members; the National Association of Theatrical and Kine Employees, for the studio artisans; Equity, for the actors; the Film Artists Association for extras (limited by agreement with Equity to speak no more than a line of dialogue); and the Musicians' Union.

Now, to focus a little closer—a costume designer was, as an officer, protected by the ACT, whereas a wardrobe mistress came under the NATKE banner. There was no obligation for a designer to be hired on a film, but it was mandatory to have a wardrobe mistress (or master) on the crew. On tightly budgeted, self-styled films, like those made by Hammer, the former didn't figure and the latter had to assume the role. In our case, fortunately more often than not, it was Rosemary Burrows who did just that and relieved us in the production department of any worries whatsoever about costuming.

Tall and very slim, she could never be described as a great beauty in the classical sense, yet Rosemary's face is intriguing and has an inner beauty. Expressions, with merely the slightest delineation brought about by a movement of her mouth or brow, legibly convey any number of creative opinions, concerns, and successes. When we first met, I suspected she would be difficult to handle, with what initially appeared to be a sardonic air, but I could not have been more wrong. Here was a person who took her work very seriously indeed, though able to laugh about various situations, and someone who was also able to take her private life equally seriously. The unassuming Eddie Powell, her husband, was also synonymous with the company. Having the same height and build as Christopher Lee, he was the ideal stunt double for our most frequently appearing star. His appearance in many films, both for Hammer and others, usually went uncredited. But he and Rosemary were the backstop of it all. Between them they gave a vitality to everything we did.

As wardrobe mistress-cum-designer, Rosemary was responsible for countless costumes, many of great richness and others perfectly befitting the so often featured peasants of Anthony Hinds's scripts. Her style expressed depth and authenticity and her creative mind was utterly boundless.

Why, therefore, I wonder, has she not been accepted as an accredited designer, now that the closed-shop era is over? Why, today, is she still seen as a wardrobe mistress and not recognized for what she truly is—a fine costume designer equal to any who take grander credit? Inbred restrictive practices must be partly to blame, and yet maybe time has now unfairly focused on the young (and, it has to be said, the often far less talented). What Rosemary achieved on a limited budget was extraordinary, and it is that kind of a situation, of having one's back against the wall, that brings out true talent.

Demons of the Mind had a good team—cast and crew—and should be considered as one of the last first-rate pictures to come from the Hammer stable.

By now, though, long shadows had begun spreading at the end of sunny days. Hammer as we knew it was growing old. Some have looked at the leadership of Michael Carreras with questioning eyes and laid the blame at his door. But that is not fair. The truth is that fantasy had given way to "real cinema." Sam Peckinpah was grabbing audiences with *Straw Dogs,* Robert Altman brought us *M*A*S*H,* and on our own shores, Michael Caine was being hailed as a major star in such films as *Get Carter.*

From the Continent Claude Lelouch had sent us *Un Homme et une Femme* and American Chinese actor Bruce Lee was pulling in the crowds.

Yet it was not quite all over. Jimmy Sangster had one more trick up his clever sleeve.

· 11 ·

Lengthening Shadows

"*You're* fired." This time it wasn't Bette Davis, but another actress speaking.

The recipient of this news, who was standing close by the edge of England's M1 Motorway, was the second assistant director, Vincent Winter. Vincent was a friendly character, who, as a small child, had won an honorary Academy Award for his performance in Philip Leacock's wonderful 1953 movie *The Kidnappers*. The Oscar he was given was a special miniature version. Until he was around the age of sixteen, he had remained an actor before turning his hand to behind-the-camera roles.

He took the envelope containing the official letter, signed by me, concerning his termination of employment on *Fear in the Night,* from Judy Geeson. There was not anything sinister in this small episode, and it happened on every picture. On a Friday, two weeks before the end of shooting, and pursuant to union agreements, notice was served on all freelance employees. On this occasion we asked Judy to do the official handing out to Vincent in public, because they had enjoyed a very good, teasing kind of working relationship throughout the short filming schedule. As a well-disciplined man, he clicked his heels, saluted, and slapped her on the bottom, with "Now get along to makeup—we'll be ready to shoot in fifteen minutes." Off she went like a chastened schoolgirl, an affirmation of their shared good humor.

What made the situation even more laughable was that this picture was filmed in a total of twenty days, and the crew had barely begun work before they received notice of dismissal. They all knew it was coming, and hiring them on one simple four-week contract could have saved quite a lot of ink and paper. But nothing as obvious as that existed.

The quarter of an hour Vincent had given Judy to ready herself was quite a short time, but at the age of twenty-four, she would be certain to emerge from her trailer looking as pretty as a picture. However, fifteen minutes for Joan Collins, who played our other female lead, would never have sufficed. No matter, she was not on this particular location. Joan had enjoyed some success as an ingénue, but by this time had reached the difficult patch in her career that comes to almost everyone. As it happened, we were very lucky to get her before she took off and shot to the very top. As a person she was demanding, although I do not say it as a criticism. She would work people around her hard, but she equally drove herself. I should add that Joan looked a million dollars in every shot.

Jimmy Sangster and Michael Carreras had been good chums for many a year, and both wanted Hammer to move with the tide. Jimmy was progressing toward the psychological drama. While supporting this, Michael's efforts went into pulling in any direction against the gothic horror, so they once again found themselves on the same track. And Jimmy had a new script to fit the bill. Well, it wasn't exactly new, and he even told me he had filmed different versions of it before. It followed a line very similar to Henri Clouzot's 1955 film, *Les Diaboliques*. No matter; it's a well-used theme and has appeared in various guises countless times before and since. Michael put together a double bill with *Fear in the Night* as the junior entrant and *Straight on Till Morning*, starring Rita Tushingham, at the top of the bill (Peter Collinson was its director).

With the new-look Hammer, there was a flurry of activity and, as head of production, Roy Skeggs was kept pretty busy and consequently not to be seen around our film much. And, as Jimmy was to direct, he had little time to attend to the producer's chores, so happily these fell almost totally to me. In the past, especially during my Tigon days, I had assumed the task by default and so already had some experience. Added to this was the fact that production managers were much more creatively involved in the making of a film then than they are now. Each day I would run rushes with the editors, view rough cuts, and approve sets and attend casting sessions—in this instance not many. Hammer worked to a formula, so the preparation of the final budget, made from Roy's draft, was a comparatively simple piece of work. Starting with the bottom-line figure of some £120,000, I worked back to the top, the whole thing taking just half a day to complete. (I still chuckle about the entry for extras, which amounted to fourteen pounds—*Fear in the Night* was an intimate film!)

We did not shoot at Elstree Studios at all but in and around a country house a few miles away. There was a tremendous advantage to this, because union rules demanded that filming on a stage had to finish promptly at 5:20 P.M., whereas on location this could be stretched by anything up to a couple of hours without causing the unit to become irritable. In reality we would usually wrap at around six and the rest of the day was ours. Often my new girlfriend, Caroline, who was also my production secretary, and I would have dinner with Jimmy and his wife at the White Elephant Club in London's Curzon Street and frequently meet up with Peter Collinson and his girlfriend, also a Caroline. There we would swap stories about the development of our shared double bill. Unlike Seth Holt, Peter had already made his definitive film, *The Italian Job*, in 1969. I must not dwell too much on Peter, because I never worked with him, but he was known for his toughness with cast and crew and was considered by some to be imperious. To me he couldn't have been friendlier.

Our picture, which focused on an already disturbed young woman (Judy Geeson) in jeopardy, had Peter Cushing as the apparent antagonist. There was a nice twist when it is revealed that her new husband (played by Ralph Bates) and Molly Carmichael (Joan Collins as Cushing's wife) were the real villains. Although quite effectively handled, the film does not really hold up today, probably because it is over-simplistic, with only a few characters in the mix. Also it is confined to the environs of a private school during the vacation period. In an attempt to open it up, I suggested to Jimmy that a scene in which Bates and Geeson stop for a picnic lunch, on their way to what will become her new home in the country, be done on a location different from the readily available woods. My idea was to put them in a wayside restaurant on a motorway, where speeding cars could be seen through the windows—an absolute contrast to the tranquil surroundings to come.

"We can't afford it," said Jimmy.

"Why not?" I countered.

"The nearest place is fifty miles up the road and we've only got half a day on the schedule."

"Motorway—fifty miles—a little over an hour away for the slowest vehicle. We leave base at seven-fifteen—start shooting by nine—finish by lunchtime—back to base after a short break—and you'll be up and running again by three."

"Well, if you think we can do it, I'm with you," he said.

We went there on the following Friday, and so that's why Vincent Winter was standing on the noisy verge of the M1 when he was given his notice of dismissal.

Pushing the boat out a degree or two was an essential part of making these low-cost films—somehow, somewhere we had to find a wide moment. Not that I am seriously suggesting such a location can be considered big under normal circumstances, but for a story set in a few largely empty rooms and a garden, it did offer up a touch of contrast. The point is that the principle is sound, albeit relative. We did our best on an extremely modest budget.

During the third week I saw a problem with the rushes. Thanks to my camera days, I was able to pick up the most minute flaws.

"Can you run them again," I said to the editors; it wasn't a question.

"Why?" they asked, innocently enough.

"There's something wrong."

They complied with my request.

"There," I exclaimed.

"Where?"

"Around every four seconds."

We started running the footage yet again.

"There!"

They could not see the problem.

"I'll click my fingers just as it happens."

Rhythmically, one frame in some ninety-six was photographically slightly underexposed. At last the others concurred with what I'd pointed out.

Several explanations were possible. Eastman Kodak's raw stock could have had a manufacturing blemish. The camera department might have had a blip in the running speed of the camera, or the laboratories had a mechanical problem in the processing plant. I got on the phone, only to hear a consistent response: "Not our department. Can't possibly be us."

"Not us! You've obviously got a film problem."

The following day, with the same flaw evident, I insisted on an assembly in the projection room of the important gentlemen who headed each department. They all arrived, no doubt concerned that they would have to field the responsibility of an insurance claim. And along came the Kodak representative (willing if necessary to change our consignment of film) and our contact at Technicolor.

"Thank you for coming. You've all heard about the trouble. We will run the footage and I will do the same as I did yesterday and anticipate the flaw by clicking my fingers."

They all saw it immediately.

"I'm not here to accuse," I said at the end. "That is entirely unimportant—it's simply that we have to get the matter sorted out and one of your departments can do that. Discuss it between yourselves and give me a call with the answer." At that point I left the theater, hoping I was making an honest rather than pretentious exit, because the only thing of concern to me was the good of our little film.

Barely thirty minutes later, the sound department called. "It's down to us." As peculiar as it may seem, the sound department was responsible for powering the camera's motor. "Variable speeds in the drives."

That was technical stuff beyond my understanding, but speeding the camera up for a fraction of a second had caused the underexposure of certain frames of film.

"Can you sort it out?"

"Yes... immediately," said the voice at the other end of the receiver. "What about an insurance claim?" was querulously added.

"I think we can probably cut around the dodgy bits."

This event is related solely as an illustration of how seriously we took the quality of our end product. The truth of the matter is that we could have gotten away with it. But getting away with it was not acceptable.

The December chill started to bite severely during the final week, and fogs rolled in by three each afternoon. Great effect was naturally created for the night exterior scenes, but they took their toll on cameraman

Arthur Grant. An acute asthma-sufferer-cum-smoker, he was working in life-threatening conditions. I persuaded him to remain in the warmth of the house as the camera was set up for each shot and the electricians maneuvered the arc lights into position. But as a true professional, he insisted on going outside to view the scene through the lens before giving his approval. *Fear in the Night* was the last picture shot by Hammer's stalwart cinematographer.

Other sad recollections come from this time; Peter Collinson died at the age of forty-four; Vincent Winter, who went on to have a short but successful career as a production manager on films such as *Indiana Jones and the Temple of Doom*, died at fifty-one, as did Ralph Bates. Probably he will best be remembered for his starring role in the television series of *Poldark*.

Mutiny on the Buses was next. All went smoothly enough, and the box office receipts were again very good. It was fun to work on, but it is still not a high point in my working life. Reg Varney, an End of the Pier vaudevillian type of performer, again brought the more vulgar British humor to life with great adeptness, as did his fellow actors, but in the end this was a formula film, produced solely to earn money.

Yet, in spite of the gallant efforts of Michael Carreras and Roy Skeggs, Hammer continued to slip away.

"Ah, my dear boy," said Terry Fisher as he put his hand on my shoulder. "It's so good to see you."

Terry, now recovered as much as he ever would be from his second victimization by a road vehicle, had been coaxed back by Roy to do what was to be a final stint with the company—*Frankenstein and the Monster from Hell*.

Although many of the trimmings were up to standard, ultimately this was not a very good story about the evil baron. The fault starts with the script—invariably the real reason for any film's failure—and too little money. And although the monster's appearance showed great imagination, in the end it looked silly, and any sympathy one might have had for it was diluted. Dave Prowse, an enormous gymnast, filled the boots and was at the outset of a career in which he would be dressed in disguises that made him unrecognizable. They wouldn't even reveal his face at the end of *Star Wars*, in which he played Darth

Vader. He's a nice and unassuming man who has suffered too much for his art.

Our Frankenstein movie had quite a large cast, headed by Peter Cushing, of course. Ever the gentleman, he clearly still suffered from the loss of Helen but never let his personal thoughts intrude on others. In the end he outlived her by twenty-three years and played many more parts in many more films—a bonus for millions of cinema-goers.

Madeline Smith was the principal girl and was, in my view, the prettiest of all the leading ladies. Soft-spoken and of gentle mien, she was remarkably easy to work with.

The picture editor was James Needs. He had been employed by the company for many years as supervising editor and generally operated out of the old Hammer House on Wardour Street. Only occasionally was this remote man seen at any of the studios, and it wasn't until this time round that I got to know him. Tall and with a genuine sparkle of humor beneath the surface, he was a fine storyteller. Because of cost-cutting, he no longer had editors to supervise and so found himself back in a hands-on world. This was to be the last movie he worked on. The same applied to Terry Fisher.

And it was my final job with the company as well. I never expected it to be—it was just the way things panned out. My loyalty was as strong as ever, and I know this was reciprocated.

Spring 1972. Tony Keys called and offered me the job as production manager on the film he was to make for Rank. Unwisely I declined, in favor of a better financial offer (with alimony to pay and school fees creeping up, I had to go where the money was): a disastrous piece of work for EMI called *Our Miss Fred* starring the female impersonator, Danny La Rue, who was, in fact, a very good actor. It was a misery to make from the production side because the ample schedule was never met and each day we drifted more and more behind. Despite my ongoing warnings to the company executives that we would go well over budget, nothing was done by them to remedy the situation—like a couple of sackings at a senior level. What was unforgivable was that some of the executives were even amused by the situation. The result for me was that I was forever undoing arrangements and resetting them up—such a waste of time, money, and energy.

Only once in the thirty years since then has a film been quite as miserable for me in that way. I'm not saying I want everything to be easy, and in fact the tougher a film gets to make, the more fun it can be. An example of this came in 1982 on a series we made in the U.K. for CBS that was sideswiped by six weeks of blizzards. The schedule went topsy-turvy in a major way. One day, when the weather eased up a fraction, we had five directors on the same location snatching scenes from their individual episodes. It was a bit like being blindfolded and standing on a tightrope in a tempest and trying to juggle with bars of soap!

But everyone was pulling together on that series in just the same way they pulled together at Hammer. That's the most important thing of all.

Afterword

Unquestionably Hammer Films advanced the careers of many to the level of international household names—the most obvious being Christopher Lee, Peter Cushing, Oliver Reed, Raquel Welch, and Ursula Andress. It revived the careers of others such as Joan Collins, Jack Palance, Bette Davis, and Tallulah Bankhead, as well as the great Paul Robeson. Many of the most solid of British actors were kept in employment—Andrew Keir, Michael Ripper, Felix Aylmer, Eric Porter, Michael Medwin, Robert Morley, Martita Hunt, Freda Jackson, Yvonne Mitchell, and literally hundreds more. One of the first rungs on the ladder was given to the likes of Simon Ward and others, including a young actor called Christopher Neame.

It was around the time of *Blood from the Mummy's Tomb* that I became aware of the newcomer. Michael Whitehall was his agent. I phoned him, "Michael, about your client. Don't you think he should change his name? If he doesn't there's going to be confusion."

"I don't see why. Besides, it's what he was born with and he is going to keep it," he said adamantly.

And that was that. Neame is not a common name, and in fact all Neames are related. So there we had two cousins, removed by three, four, or five times, working for the same company.

A few weeks later, on my return from a location to Elstree Studios, I received a message from the reception desk. "Please telephone Michael Whitehall." I did so.

"Ah," he said, "I think there has been some confusion. I wanted the other one."

"I told you it would happen!"

And it has been happening ever since. Frequently I'm told that somebody heard me on the radio a couple of weeks past—or has seen me in some film.

When the other one appeared as the first full-frontal nude male on television, I received mountains of fan mail (I should have charged Michael Whitehall for my time in redirecting the letters). What made me get an unlisted number was the call from a girl expressing her delight at "my" performance. I spent quite a while explaining the truth, and she still ended up by saying, "I still think you were excellent in the part."

But even so, I had no intention of adapting my appellation. Not for me a Roy Ward Baker outcome. So there's a message for all Hammer aficionados—don't look for me in front of the camera in *Lust for a Vampire* or *Dracula AD 1972*—you won't see me.

Michael Carreras struggled bravely on throughout the seventies and into the early eighties, and more and more bare-breasted girls appeared on the screen in the hope of attracting an audience. I'm sure they helped, but in the end it was no good. Roy Skeggs and the dapper Brian Lawrence bought Hammer Films from him in 1982. They produced a couple of TV series with the generic title *Hammer House of Horrors* that were of a pretty good standard. By then I had lost contact with Roy—not for any reason other than that we were moving in different directions.

Mine was to start as a production supervisor with a Canadian/British company, and on one of the productions with them, I met the man who was to become my business partner for the next twenty years and more. Together director Henry Herbert and I made the first film I produced. *Emily* (a sex picture), starring Koo Stark, was to cause quite a storm shortly after its release because of her reported relationship with Prince Andrew. Subsequently moving on, often with Henry, further producing jobs were to come my way. Three of them were with John Hawkesworth: *Danger UXB, The Flame Trees of Thika* (both for Euston Films—the latter with old friend Roy Stannard from Metro days as the set designer), and *QED* (the show sideswiped by the blizzard) with Sam Waterston and another old chum, Julian Glover, from *Quatermass*. Two pictures were from Jack Rosenthal scripts, the memorable *The Knowledge*, about the learning experience of a group of would-be London taxi drivers, and *Bye, Bye Baby*. My personal favourite was *Monsignor Quixote*, starring Alec Guinness and Leo McKern, which I scripted from the Graham Greene novel. Several other films followed, and then, in 1994, along came my second misery production. It is wise not to go into the problems surrounding it here; suffice it to say that, although perfectly capable of making excellent films, the producing company did not operate according to the school of Hammer. To be fair, why should they have done? They had their own set of rules.

Just as people ask what a director does, a similar question is often asked about a producer. "They raise the money," is the usual answer. Well, I'd have to say yes and no about that. Raising money is only part of the job, and very often a producer will be involved with it only peripherally. His or her absolute main function is to oversee those aspects of a film that involve running it smoothly and efficiently on the way to the final polished product. Also, the producer has to be the director's ally, so a good sense of storytelling is an essential requirement for giving low-profile aid. A producer is a maître d' to the director, who is the chef. Another essential is for everyone to have complete and utter trust in the producer, who in return must make sure that the employees are given due praise and dignity. An additional ability is to pre-judge the reaction of others to a given situation—but maybe this is becoming too subtle. Actually to produce a film at last gives one the added bonus of receiving a paid advertising credit on the poster. In the end, though, credit is unimportant. The important thing is the satisfaction of having cleared the way for the making of a good film. That's all that matters.

In 1998 I did something very different altogether. I met a young composer by the name of Ethan Lewis Maltby and fulfilled a lifelong ambition by writing the book and lyrics for a stage musical. *Courtenay* premiered in July 2002 and is set to go on tour as I write. A bonus is that Roy Stannard is the set designer. Ethan is destined to join the ranks of household names. Although there is no camera crew on the production (other than a broadcast crew for one performance), it is a wonderful reminder of the glorious years I spent in the family atmosphere of Bray and Elstree. Often, when faced with a difficulty, I turn to the remedy ANK would have prescribed—clearly thinking it through.

Happily, and largely because of this book, I have re-met Roy Skeggs and we enjoy lunching together in London. He is a good man, who, as a fellow alumnus, misses the camaraderie of long gone days.

In 2000 he sold the company, and it is still extant. How could it be otherwise? It owns an extensive library of films that will continue to run on television or be released to the public on videos and DVDs.

Countless times the grapevine has buzzed with news that Hammer is to re-make many of its classic titles with big names attached. I, for one, hope this will never come to be, because the gothic horrors, in particular, were of a given time, ergo, definitive. But, to argue the other way, what is *Lord of the Rings*? And look who's in it—Christopher Lee, now in his eighties and still in top form. That said, too often filmmakers' attempts to re-shoot earlier work have foundered, and it is astonishing that none have seen it coming. Take, for example, remakes of David Lean's *Brief Encounter* and *Great Expectations*; take the more recent versions of William Wyler's *Wuthering Heights* and even Laurence Olivier's *Henry V*.

By moving outside the genre of archetypal Hammer films, remakes might prove acceptable because they would not be associated with the company. But in that case why don't producers simply start from scratch on those types of subjects? As previously noted, *Fear in the Night* is a sort of version of Clouzot's film. And there are other, non-gothic, potentially good projects in Hammer's vaults that need not necessarily bear the company's name as a marketing strategy; *Quatermass* is an obvious example. The fans of the company are numerous, but today only a few of the public in general will understand what "The House of Horror" was all about.

Let sleeping dogs lie; God bless them all, too.

Appendix

Christopher Neame's Films with Hammer

(Actual Production Dates)

Date	Original and Subsequent Titles	Neame's role
1965	Dracula—Prince of Darkness *The Bloody Scream of Dracula* *Disciple of Dracula* *Dracula 3, Revenge of Dracula*	clapper boy★
1965	Rasputin—The Mad Monk	clapper boy★
1966	Prehistoric Women *Slave Girls*	anamorphic focus assistant★
1966	The Witches *The Devil's Own*	third assistant director★
1966	Frankenstein Created Woman *Frankenstein Made Woman*	third assistant director★
1966	The Mummy's Shroud	second assistant director★
1967	Quatermass and the Pit *Five Million Years to Earth* *The Mind Benders*	second assistant director★
1967	The Anniversary	second assistant director★
1967	The Devil Rides Out *The Devil's Bride*	second assistant director★ and second unit director★
1968	Journey to the Unknown *Out of the Unknown*	unit manager

1969	Frankenstein Must Be Destroyed	production manager
1971	Blood from the Mummy's Tomb	production manager and second unit director★
1971	On the Buses	production manager
1971	Demons of the Mind *Blood Evil* *Blood Will Have Blood* *Nightmare of Terror*	production manager
1971	Fear in the Night *Dynasty of Fear* *Honeymoon of Fear*	production manager
1972	Mutiny on the Buses	production manager
1972	Frankenstein and the Monster from Hell	production manager

★ uncredited

Index

Allen, Patrick, 57
Altman, Robert, 110
Ambler, Eric, 70, 82
Anderson, Lindsay, 3
Anderson, Pam, 90
Andress, Ursula, 121
Arrighi, Niké, 57
Ashton, Roy, 9
Aylmer, Felix, 121

Baker, Roy Ward, 33–36, 42, 49–51, 73, 122
Banerjee, Victor, 2
Bankhead, Tallulah, 121
Banks, Arthur, 9
Barron, Roderick, 98
Bates, Ralph, 115, 118
Batt, Bert, 35, 36, 40, 42, 45, 50, 55, 59, 62, 67, 68, 85, 86
Baxter, Stanley, 3
Bayley, Dick, 60, 61
Bernard, James, 13
Beswick, Martine, 19
Binney, Neil, 101
Bloch, Robert, 74
Bogarde, Dirk, 2, 3
Booth, Harry, 104
Bowie, Les, 9, 29, 62, 88

Bowles, Peter, 108
Brandy, Howard, 96
Briant, Shane, 106
Burrows, Rosemary, 9, 28, 108–10

Caine, Michael, 110
Canning, Victor, 53
Carey, Tristram, 43
Carlson, Veronica, 86, 87
Carreras, Christopher, 68, 69
Carreras, Enrico, 72
Carreras, James, 10, 52, 94
Carreras, Jo, 103
Carreras, Michael 10, 18, 100, 101, 103, 110, 114, 118, 122
Carstairs, John Paddy, 11
Chaffey, Don, 79
Christie, Julie, 3
Close, Ivy, 1
Clouzot, Henri, 114, 124
Coe, Peter, 67
Collins, Joan, 114, 115, 121
Collinson, Peter, 114, 115, 118
Cossins, James, 47, 50
Cotten, Joseph, 75–77
Couloris, George, 96
Coward, Noël, 1
Cowlard, Albert, 5, 7

Crutchley, Rosalie, 96
Cushing, Helen, 89, 97, 119
Cushing, Peter, 12, 16, 25, 86, 87, 89, 96, 97, 115, 119, 121

Danziger Brothers, 36
Davis, Bette, 21, 45–54, 96, 121
de Havilland, Olivia, 22
Delgado, Roger, 29
Denberg, Susan, 24, 26
Deutsch, David, 68
Dineen, Sue, 67
Donald, James, 37, 42

Faithfull, Marianne, 106
Farmer, Suzan, 14
Faulkener, John, 65
Ffrangcon Davies, Gwen, 22, 57
Finch, Peter, 2
Fisher, Terrence, 6, 7, 9, 12, 24, 33, 55, 57, 64–66, 86, 89, 90, 118, 119
Fleischmann, Jack, 71, 74, 75
Fontaine, Joan, 21, 22
Forbes, Bryan, 96, 97
Frankel, Cyril, 22

Geeson, Judy, 113–15
Gibson Mary, 47
Gilling, John, 9, 29–31
Glover, Julian, 38, 40, 43, 122
Godden, Norman, 2
Godwin, Frank, 105, 106
Godwin, Harold, 87
Grant, Arthur, 9, 23, 30, 31, 118
Grant, Moray, 9, 26, 27, 36 77
Gray, Charles, 57
Greene, Graham, 52, 90, 122
Greene, Leon, 57, 58
Guinness, Alec, 1, 25, 90, 122

Haffenrichter, Oswald, 96, 103
Hancock, Sheila, 47, 50

Hardy, Robert, 106
Harlow, Pauline, 9, 29
Harris, Graham, 93
Harris, Julie, 75
Harris, Richard, 3
Harrison (Ambler), Joan, 70, 71, 74, 75, 82
Hawkesworth, John, 34, 122
Hedley, Jack, 47, 50
Hemmings, David, 93
Hepburn, Katharine, 2
Herbert, Henry, 122
Hermes, Doug, 25
Hill, Bluey, 27–31, 80
Hills, Gillian, 106
Hinds, Anthony, 10, 11, 30, 32, 68, 69, 71–74, 81, 82, 89
Hinds (Hammer), Will, 71, 72
Hitchcock, Alfred, 70, 75
Holt, Sally, 96, 99, 102
Holt, Seth, 95, 96, 98–100, 108
Hope, Bob, 2
Hordern, Michael, 106–8
Horton, Michael, 53
Hunt, Martita, 121
Hyman, Sally, 98

Jackson, Freda, 121
Jones, Freddie, 86

Keir, Andrew, 12, 37, 42, 97, 121
Kelly, James, 93
Keys, Basil, 11
Keys, "Bunch," 11, 81
Keys, Roddy, 11
Kimberley, Maggie, 32
King, Nosmo, 72
Kneale, Nigel, 22, 36
Kubrick, Stanley, 36

La Rue, Danny, 119
Lacey, Catherine, 29, 75

Lamb, Irene, 9, 65
Lamont, Duncan, 22, 43
Lawrence, Brian, 10, 122
Le Fanu, J. Sheridan, 91
Leacock, Philip, 113
Lean, David, 1, 21, 124
Lee, Bruce, 111
Lee, Christopher, 7, 12, 15, 16, 17, 56, 57, 90, 121, 124
Lelouch, Claude, 111
Leon, Valerie, 98, 102
Lewis, Ian, 60, 61
Lloyd, Norman, 75
Loussier, Jacques, 91

Macgregor, Scott, 98
MacIlwraith, Bill, 45
Magee, Patrick, 106
Maltby, Ethan Lewis, 123
Marsh, Laurie, 92, 93
Martell, Philip, 13
Matheson, Richard, 59
Matthews, Francis, 14
McKern, Leo, 122
McNaught, Bob, 11
Medwin, Michael, 121
Middlemass, Frank, 87
Mills, Hayley, 34
Mitchell, Yvonne, 106, 121
Mitchum, Robert, 3
Monroe, Marilyn, 49
Morell, André, 32
Morely, Robert, 121
Morris, Aubrey, 98
Morris, Oswald, 5
Mrs. T, 32

Neame, Beryl, 70
Neame, Christopher (not the author), 121
Neame, Elwin, 1
Neame, Emma, 94, 102

Neame, Gareth, 41, 102
Neame, Heather, 5, 16, 23, 31, 35, 38, 39, 40, 69, 92, 94, 99
Neame, Ronald, 1, 3, 11, 54, 60, 79, 88, 104
Neame, Shuna, 73, 102
Needs, James, 119
Nelson Keys, Anthony, 6, 9, 11, 12, 16–19, 23, 30, 33, 35, 43, 55, 57, 58, 63–65, 67, 68, 69, 81, 82, 85–89, 119, 123, 124
Nelson Keys, Maggie, 68, 81, 90
Newman, Sydney, 49
North, Norman, 40

Olivier, Laurence, 5, 93, 124

Palance, Jack, 121
Parkyn, Leslie, 2
Partleton, George, 47
Peck, Gregory, 2, 48
Peckinpah, Sam, 110
Phillips, Leslie, 3
Polanski, Roman, 92
Porter, Eric, 121
Powell, Eddie, 9, 65, 110
Powell, Michael, 2
Prowse, David, 118, 119

Rakoff, Alvin, 46, 49, 50, 57, 58
Randall, Tony, 16
Rawkins, Ken, 14, 15
Reed, Carol, 96
Reed, Michael, 4, 5, 9, 16
Reed, Oliver, 95, 121
Reid, Beryl, 93
Ripper, Michael, 12, 32, 121
Roberts, Mike, 18
Roberts, Rachel, 3
Robertson Justice, James, 3
Robeson, Paul, 121

Robinson, Bernard, 9, 13, 14, 24, 31, 37, 86–88
Robson, Flora, 93
Roeg, Nicholas, 17
Rosenthal, Jack, 122
Rubber, Viola, 46–49
Rutter, Mike, 5

Sangster, Jimmy, 42, 45, 49, 52, 53, 59, 111, 114–16
Scott, Richard, 65
Sellers, Peter, 3
Sharp, Don, 9, 13, 51
Shelley, Barbara, 14, 16, 37, 42
Silk, Geoff, 61, 62
Silk, Jack, 61, 62
Sister Basil, 39–41
Skeggs, Roy, 76, 92, 93, 95, 96, 98–101, 106, 114, 118, 122, 123
Smith, Madeline, 119
Smith, Maggie, 2, 5
Stannard, Roy, 79, 122, 123
Stark, Koo, 122
Stewart, Estelle, 73
Stoker, Bram, 87, 96
Stringer, Michael, 106, 107
Style, Michael, 91
Suschitzky, Peter, 67
Sykes, Peter, 107, 108
Symonds, Dusty, 35

Talbot, Ken, 77
Tenser, Tony, 90–94
Thatcher, Margaret, 55
Thomas, Ralph, 5
Thompson, J. Lee, 105
Towers, Harry Alan, 17
Tushingham, Rita, 114

Unsworth, Geoffrey, 5

Varney, Reg, 103, 118
Villiers, James, 96
Vivian, Bert, 65

Walsh, Kay, 11, 21, 81, 82
Walters, Thorley, 12
Ward, Simon, 86, 121
Waterman, Dennis, 91
Waterston, Sam, 122
Waxman, Harry, 46, 47, 50
Welch, Raquel, 121
Welles, Orson, 75
Wheatley, Dennis, 56
Whitehall, Michael, 121, 122
Wicking, Christopher, 105
Williams, Frank, 38
Winter, Vincent, 113–16, 118
Wintle, Julian, 2
Wisdom, Norman, 2
Wyler, William, 124

About the Author

Christopher Neame's roots are firmly embedded in the film industry. The third of four generations in the business, he worked on films such as *The Anniversary* starring Bette Davis, *The Wrong Arm of the Law* with Peter Sellers, and Lindsay Anderson's *This Sporting Life* with Richard Harris. Moving to Hammer films, at Bray Studios, in the mid-1960s, he was involved with many of the company's cult gothic movies. Subsequently as a producer, he has been responsible for the production of films and series such as *Bellman and True, Foreign Body, Danger UXB, The Knowledge, The Flame Trees of Thika, The Irish R.M.*, and *QED*, with Sam Waterston in the lead role.

Christopher has several screenplays to his credit, including Graham Greene's *Monsignor Quixote*, starring Alec Guinness, which Christopher also produced, and H. E. Bates's *Feast of July* for Buena Vista. More recently he has turned his hand to the stage musical, writing the book and lyrics for *Courtenay*, which received its U.K. première in 2002 and tours during the summer of 2003. He is married and lives in a small country village near the city of Canterbury.

OHIO UNIVERSITY LIBRARY

Please return this book as soon as you have finished with it. In order to avoid a fine it must be returned by the latest date stamped below. All books are subject to recall after two weeks or immediately if needed for reserve.

CF